COMPREHENSIVE PLANNING
General Theory and Principles

Books by the Same Author

Federal Aids to Local Planning (Editor), 1941
Urban Planning and Public Opinion, 1942
Aerial Photography in Urban Planning and Research, 1948
The Corporate Planning Process, 1962
Selected References for Corporate Planning 1966
Planning: Aspects and Applications, 1966
Comprehensive Urban Planning: A Selective Annotated
    Bibliography with Related Materials, 1970
City Planning and Aerial Information, 1971
Urban Air Traffic and City Planning: Case Study of Los
    Angeles County, 1973
Planning Urban Environment, 1974, Russian Edition, 1979
Urban Planning Theory (Editor), 1975
Comparative Urban Design, Rare Engravings, 1830—1843, 1978
Continuous City Planning: Integrating Municipal
    Management and City Planning, 1981

COMPREHENSIVE PLANNING
General Theory and Principles

Melville C. Branch

Professor of Planning
University of Southern California

Illustrated by the Author

PALISADES PUBLISHERS
Pacific Palisades, California 90272-0744

Library of Congress Catalog Card Number: 83–061680
International Standard Book Number: 0-913530–32–8

Palisades Publishers
P. O. Box 744
Pacific Palisades, California 90272-0744

Printed in the United States of America

Library of Congress Cataloging in Publication Data

Branch, Melville Campbell, 1913–
    Comprehensive planning.

    Bibliography: p.
    Includes index.
    1. Planning.   I. Title.
HD87.5.B72 1983   658.4'012   82-61680
ISBN 0-913530-32-8

CONTENTS

FOREWORD

HISTORICALLY THE THREE MAJOR applications of planning have been considered separately in both theory and practice: civil governmental planning for cities and regions, business planning, and military planning. There has been little contact between those concerned with each of these applications, except for military engineers designing the peripheral defenses of cities in the past, defense contractors producing military weapons today, and a few urban and regional planners employed by land developers, utility companies, and financial institutions. There is even less intercommunication with respect to theory, principles, and practice.

The author's experience with these primary areas of planning and his lifetime study of planning as an organized endeavor have convinced him that the process of planning is basically the same in all its applications. There are, of course, great differences between the organizational entities that engage in planning. A civil government and a private business enterprise are very different indeed: in their constituent populations, objectives, governance, legal powers, and in almost every other way. Military units are the most distinct: with their chain of command and absolute control, unique operational characteristics brought about by the transcending objective of national survival, and overriding powers justified by the emergency conditions of war.

Despite these differences, the basic procedural steps are the same in each case: (1) collection of descriptive and prescriptive information, (2) analysis of this information, (3) reaching conclusions and making decisions, (4) designation and effectuation of implementing actions, and (5) comparison of the results of planning with its intentions, and corresponding adjustment or revision as indicated.

A limited number of techniques are available for carrying out these basic procedural steps. Information is commonly collected by numerical count, scientific experiment, sample survey, remote sensing, physical measurement, structured judgment, or subjective observation. Only a limited number of mathematical, statistical, cost comparison, logical, and judgmental techniques are available for analytical correlation and projection.

Similarly, basic ways of reaching rational conclusions and making decisions are comparable the world over. The individual may reach a conclusion and decision by accepting and acting on what available information reveals, by requiring additional or different data and analysis, or by relying on subjective judgment, emotional reaction, random chance, or even best guess. Groups may conclude and decide by developing a consensus, collective compromise, adversary proceedings, majority vote, hierarchial or autocratic determination.

All actions implementing planning require a necessary degree of specification, consideration of incremental actions and events and their interaction, intervals of time for various accomplishments, and instruments of effectuation which can be used to perform the prescribed actions. Various ways of indicating a sequence or schedule of progressive accomplishment have been developed, ranging from a simple listing casually conceived to complicated calculative methods.

The author's motivation to undertake this initial formulation concerning theory and principles springs from his conviction of the inevitability of planning in human affairs, and the absolute necessity of organized forethought for the advancement of the human condition and the survival of the human species, discussed in the chapter on the Theoretical Context of comprehensive planning. If this process is as crucial as the author believes, it is important to identify and apply a general theory and universal principles of comprehensive planning.

The sixteen principles identified in this book are discussed at sufficient introductory length to indicate their primary characteristics and the more important considerations to be taken into account in their application. Each is a basic and complex subject in itself, represented in the literature by extensive documentation dealing with various aspects of the subject. Each of these principles deserves a book expanding specifically on its application to comprehensive planning.

This initial formulation can only be expressed in words: carefully selected and employed to comprise a clear and precise statement. To prevent misunderstanding and promote consistent use, key words are defined at the beginning of the book and at the beginning of each section. In the future it should be possible to augment written expression with some form of nonverbal abstraction.

As they are in all fields of knowledge, theory and principles are part of education in urban, regional, business, military, and other kinds of planning. "Basic truths" affect how planning is approached and how it is performed in practice. Identification of theory and principles also elucidates the nature of comprehensive planning for the fields closely related to this endeavor: business management, public administration, economics, political science, sociology, law, several fields of engineering, architecture, and landscape architecture. This volume can serve as an introductory textbook and basis for discussion in planning education and as a reference for related fields.

Consider the auk;
Becoming extinct because he forgot how to fly, and
could only walk.
Consider man, who may well become extinct
Because he forgot how to walk and learned how to fly
before he thinked.

Ogden Nash, 1952

One
EXPLANATION OF
ESSENTIAL TERMS

THE TERMS EMPLOYED IN science are carefully defined, or experimental conditions are described precisely when they are not so uniformly understood that simple reference to an established terminology or technique is enough. Mathematical formulations are accompanied by the definitions necessary for clarity and consistent understanding. Careful use of language and precise specification of conditions promote progressive advancement of knowledge by different people at different times.

The meaning, comparability, and usefulness of much of the planning literature today are severely limited by inconsistent use of terms. Because these terms are defined differently by different people, readers must repeatedly readjust their minds to each different definition of the same terminology. Theoretical and prescriptive formulations cannot be derived one from another or substituted one for another without distractive translation or substitution of terms.

Despite this confusing situation, certain terms must be used repeatedly in formulating and discussing principles of comprehensive planning. There are no equivalent or substitute terms, nor are there now other means of adequate descriptive statement. The following definitions and explanations serve the purposes of this initial formulation of general theory and planning principles. They could be adopted as linguistic "building blocks" in the continuing study of comprehensive planning.*

*Parts of these definitions and explanations are drawn from: Melville C. Branch and Ira M. Robinson, "Goals and Objectives in Civil Comprehensive Planning," *The Town Planning Review,* January 1968, pp. 261–274.

An *organism* is an animate or inanimate entity, activity, or other structural or organizational unity: "any thing or structure composed of distinct parts and so constructed that the functioning of the parts and their relation to one another is governed by their relation to the whole."

Although all organisms operate within progressively larger contexts until ultimately a global or even galactic level of consideration is reached, each has an identity and operational distinctiveness of its own. This is the result of evolutionary or historical development, institutional identification, legal jurisdiction, or some geologic, geographical, economic, social, military, or other self-determination or particularity. Animate organisms have the capability to affect their future state within the larger context of which they are part.

An organism may be governmental jurisdiction, private enterprise, military unit, association, society, project: any organizational, operational, spatial,or other entity which has some directive mechanism. This can range from the formal managerial structure of a government or business enterprise to the nebulous operational arrangement of a family or the evolutionary forces within an animal or biological organism of nature.

The functional characteristics of an organism comprise its *structure:* the "arrangement of parts, of organs, or of constituent tissues or particles, in a substance or body—the interrelation of parts as dominated by the general character of the whole. . . ." These include not only the physical, tangible elements of the organism, but its psychological, social, cultural, and other characteristics as well. It is the structure of the organism that is both the object and means of planning comprehensively.

System is sometimes preferred to organism as a descriptive term, particularly by engineers.

Planning (or to plan) is the process of directing human activities and natural forces with reference to the future. It is continuous, since plans are formulated and realized only to be replaced by others which have been adjusted to the changes constantly occurring. Paraphrasing Alfred North Whitehead: "The process itself is the actuality." This involves identifying different elements and aspects of an organism, determining their present state and interaction, projecting them in concert throughout a period of future time, and formulating and programming a set of policies, actions, and plans to attain desired results.

Planning involves *internal actions and events* subject to complete or partial control within the organism, and those *external* to the organism over which it has little or no control. Although this distinction is not absolute for certain occurrences and situations, it serves to identify what the organism can bring about on its own initiative. A wide range of probabilities and judgments must be developed for these different actions and events, some of which are physically tangible, others comparatively intangible, some subject to meaningful quantification, others difficult or impossible to measure at present in numerical terms.

Comprehensive planning encompasses conceptually and analytically as many as possible of the essential elements of the organism which determine its course of action and influence its development, and are within the primary control of the organism itself. It is *planning for the totality* rather than for one or several of its constituent parts, system rather than subsystem planning. It incorporates the best estimates that can be made concerning pertinent events external to the organism. It does not attempt to cover every known element and aspect of the organism, but must consider the full range of its components and identify those that are most important and can be handled analytically.

The adjectives *master, general,* or *development* may be employed in civil governmental planning instead of the word comprehensive. *Corporate planning* is the term most frequently used for comprehensive planning by a company, business, or other large private enterprise. The military apply more specifically descriptive terms to their equivalent of comprehensive planning by the many different commands.

Goals, Policies, Objectives

Planning goals are general desires or intentions, whose achievement is so hopeful, distant and indefinite that they cannot be formulated and programmed with sufficient specificity to be incorporated quantitatively in the comprehensive plan. They set the general attainments toward which policies and planning objectives are broadly directed. They are sufficiently fundamental to preclude their sudden change or abandonment, but opinion concerning their relative importance may shift rapidly.

For example, city planning goals might include: a municipal economy providing full employment within the city; a physically and socially healthy urban environment; widespread and continuous public participation in local government; elimination of poverty, slums, and depressed areas. Corporate planning goals could be return on investment several times that of competitors, different products or services, or major change in managerial methods and capabilities. A goal of military planning is to emerge victorious in war or "in a better relative position" than the enemy. Although a sequence of feasible activities cannot be established today to attain long-range planning goals, opportunities will arise to move toward their realization.

Planning policies describe a desirable development and may also indicate a general approach or direction to be taken in its attainment. The way in which the policy will be executed depends on generally favorable circumstances which may develop, or on particular opportunities which occur enabling progress to be made toward the desired end. "Policy emerges when concept encounters opportunity." How it will be implemented, if at all, cannot be specifically foreseen.

To illustrate: a city planning policy could be adopted to increase the amount of affordable residential housing. Some actions to this end, such as reducing zoning restrictions against more widespread location of mobile manufactured homes, might be taken immediately if politically feasible. Other actions could be considered if opportunities arose to use less expensive residential structures, to reduce the cost of land, or to obtain subventions. Similarly, a corporation could formalize a policy of promoting greater employee participation in improving the quality of its product, not knowing exactly how it will be able to implement this policy over the years beyond a few actions to be taken immediately. An example of a policy choice for the military is whether to work toward highly sophisticated and costly weaponry and the "automated battlefield," or the larger quantities and greater reliability under battle conditions of less complex weapons available at the same cost.

Policies are instruments of planning midway between goals as defined above and objectives defined below.

A planning objective is a statement of intention that has been identified, analyzed, and expressed with sufficient specificity to indicate how it can be accomplished within the time and resources available to the organism. Insofar as any one part of the closely interconnected process of comprehensive planning can be singled out, planning objectives are the most important.

They evolve from what analysis reveals concerning the nature, needs, and potentialities of the entity for which they are developed. Demonstration of the feasibility of their attainment is an integral part of every planning objective; unless this is possible, the intention is a policy or goal rather than an objective. Most of the resources of organisms are required to maintain existing activities, to complete developments already commenced, or to undertake projects which it has been determined are needed or desired but have not yet been undertaken. Only a small fraction of the resources normally available to an organism can be applied to entirely new discretionary projects or activities.

The time period during which objectives are to be realized varies widely depending on their nature and priority. They cannot be changed so often that the minimum stability or "staying on the charted course" essential to their realization is jeopardized.

Plans and Programs

A plan is any specific formulation of purposeful activity, normally limited to a period of time or repetitive condition. It may be expressed in one or more of many forms: written statements; drawings, charts, blueprints, and other graphic representations; three-dimensional models; mathematical, statistical, and other quantitative formulations; or verbalizations expressing a plan in the mind not yet committed to paper or other more tangible form.

A comprehensive plan is a plan for an organizational entity as a whole, as distinct from a plan for one or several of its parts. It is a set of interrelated policies and sequential actions derived from continuous analysis and decision concerning the present state and future development of the organism. It is the current, adopted statement of intent, strategy, programmed accomplishment, and expected actions: periodically re-examined to determine what modification is necessary or desirable, but subject to revision or replacement whenever called for by emergency conditions or unexpected events of major import. It is a principal measure of institutional, managerial, or command performance.

A component or functional plan treats a single constituent element or functional activity of the organism. As such, it is a part of the comprehensive plan for the organism as a whole. At the same time, the component plan can be comprehensive within itself if it considers the full range of its constituent parts.

Dependent on circumstances, a plan may be comprehensive or component with respect to the next larger organizational entity. The military forces, for example, are organized into an unbroken chain of progressively larger component units culminating in a supreme command. But there are at any one time certain military units or levels within this chain of command which operate relatively independently, that is to say: plan comprehensively within strategic limits, toward designated general objectives. They may be detached to operate independently. New commands may be created which change the affiliation of units previously part of different commands. Thus, the directive of the U.S. Joint Chiefs of Staff to General Dwight D. Eisenhower during World War II "to enter the continent of Europe and, in conjunction with other Allied Nations, undertake operations aimed at the heart of Germany and the destruction of her armed forces" created a military organism which ultimately integrated the largest number of component military plans ever welded into a single comprehensive operational plan for the biggest military operation undertaken up to that time: the invasion of Normandy.

Operational plans are the specific and detailed instruments required to realize part of a comprehensive plan. They are shorter-range and finite, with a clearly predetermined beginning and end. Examples are a program and procedure of administrative reorganization within a set time, designation of the resources and activities required to manufacture a product or carry out a military operation, or the plans and specifications necessary to construct a new highway or utility system. Operational plans provide the more precise instruction and specification required to achieve a planning objective.

A subsystem plan covers several closely interdependent components. For example, in engineering, the electrical components of an automobile are treated as a subsystem because they are interrelated by their common use of electricity, and because their design requires knowledge of electrical engineering. A diversified corporation may be organized by product division, with each division responsible for its advertising, sales, production, personnel, and other components, except for a few financial limitations and policy decisions reserved for corporate management. From the viewpoint of corporate (comprehensive) planning, each such product division is a subsystem.

A planning program is the sequence of specific actions which are formulated to achieve a planning objective. They are spelled out step by step in the detail required for their effectuation. Without planning programs indicating how intentions are to be transformed into actual results for the eye to see and the hand to touch, comprehensive planning and the formulation of planning objectives are a futile exercise on paper. The existence of planning programs signifies that longer-range goals and objectives have been effectively related to the current operating situation, present realities, and the resources available.

The managerial methods of "project evaluation and review technique" (PERT), "planning, programming, and budgeting" (PPB), and "critical path scheduling" (CPS) apply to this last stage of the comprehensive planning cycle.

Analysis

Comprehensive planning analysis is the approach, method, procedure, and body of techniques employed to investigate the past and present condition of the organism, project it into the future, determine what is to be accomplished and attempted, and finally program the actions to be taken. Numerous techniques are employed, many of them developed orginally by other disciplines, but the total process of analysis, conclusion, decision, and implementation constitutes the substantive core of comprehensive planning.

Although different kinds of organisms require special knowledge and analysis fitted to their particular characteristics and requirements, there are basic similarities of approach, a sequence of study, and techniques of analysis common to the different forms or applications of planning.

A planning projection is an extension of the past and present into the future for the purposes of planning. It may be a statistical projection based on observed or derived data treated and interpreted mathematically. It may be a judgmental projection based on the structured development of expert opinion. Usually, individual projections are limited to one or several elements which can be treated with the requisite statistical reliability. All plans are composite projections in that they formulate future actions and consequent outcomes.

In this book, *a forecast is a prediction* based on subjective judgment, experiential comparison, best guess, or some other method *which does not involve statistical-mathematical analysis.*

Theory. . . .

1.a. Systematically organized knowledge applicable in a relatively wide variety of circumstances; especially, a system of assumptions, accepted principles, and rules of procedure devised to analyze, predict, or otherwise explain the nature or behavior of a specified set of phenomena.
b. Such knowledge or such a system distinguished from experiment or practice.
2. Abstract reasoning; speculation.
3. Broadly, hypothesis or supposition. . . .

Principle. . . .

1. A basic truth, law, or assumption. . .
2.a. A rule or standard. . .
3. A fixed or predetermined policy or mode of action. . .
4. A basic, or essential, quality or element determining intrinsic nature or characteristic behavior. . .
5. A rule or law concerning the functioning of natural phenomena or mechanical processes. . . .

(The American Heritage Dictionary of the English Language, 1971, pp. 1041, 1335)

Two
THEORETICAL CONTEXT

PLANNING IS SO GENERAL and so much a part of all activities that it is usually taken for granted. Because it is inconspicuous by its universal presence, *the process of planning* is seldom specifically identified and considered. Illustrations of different applications and results of planning are almost without limit. And there are multitudinous studies and research reports concerning knowledge and conditions affecting planning. But the planning process itself is rarely treated. Because it is a complex process not easily understood and often misunderstood, there is need for adequate explanation and an initial formulation of general principles. This book is devoted to this end.

However human activities are viewed, planning is everpresent. It is commonplace in everyday life: shopping for meals, provision for the education of children, career improvement, the purchase of insurance, or the very use and organization of the waking hours. Even our involuntary muscular movements reflect subconscious planning incorporated genetically in our motor reactions.

Since the earliest days of humankind planning has been inherent in personal and societal activities, recognized as essential to the conduct of government, business, and war. By the exercise of forethought to attain objectives, individuals and societies have survived and progressed. This forethought has been organized and formalized in most areas of human endeavor, and has long since been incorporated into the institutional and legal structure of society.

Most people are aware of plans by government for the location, construction, and maintenance of physical facilities they use regularly: such as highways, airways, waterways, and other transportation systems. There are plans for the conservation of natural resources, for the development of schools, hospitals, fire and police protection, water supply and sanitary systems. Public health is planned in that rules of sanitation are established, occupational hazards are regulated, food and drugs are inspected. The budgets of the various civil governments are plans for expenditure as are all other budgets. Taxes are levied and collected according to pre-established procedures. The Constitution of the United States is itself an institutional plan for representative government. As citizens of a democracy, we are constantly expressing our opinions by vote and by voice on specific plans of government ranging from a local bond issue to the federal social security system.

If a private enterprise does not plan successfully to make a profit, it will in time cease to exist. Financial plans are fundamental to business. The selection and design of products, procurement of raw materials, manufacturing, sales and advertising, packaging and distribution, cash flow and money management, and retirement systems are planned separately and in combination, to a greater or lesser extent—as are also liquidation and bankruptcy. In agriculture, the scientific farmer conducts a highly organized operation, adjusted to seasonal changes and weather forecasts, selection and rotation of crops, efficient use of labor and farm machinery, employment of fertilizers and pesticides, government estimates of total crop production, bank loans, price trends, crop storage and delivery. Every merchant and farmer engages in some planning, however different it may be in kind and degree.

In military organization, each unit from the combat team to an army is designed to function effectively as a part of the next larger unit. There are plans for command, military operation and maneuver, for supply and communication, and medical service. The very terms military tactics, strategy, and logistics define particular kinds of planning activity. To design and produce the complex weapons of modern warfare—ranging from multiple-targeted ballistic missiles and nuclear-powered submarines to hypersonic aircraft and naval aircraft carriers—requires years of sophisticated planning in each case.

Every project or effort of any size depends on organized forethought. A large building, telephone system, automobile, or bridge requires extensive architectural-engineering study and the preparation of schematics, working drawing, specifications, and production and construction schedules. Without at least a minimum of planning, such installations would not be initiated or would soon bog down in a snarl of confusion.

Since the Industrial Revolution, the age of scientific discovery has produced tremendous advances in fundamental knowledge, and made possible an impressive array of material achievements. It has contributed to deductive and inductive thought processes, provided new tools of reasoning and extended those of ancient vintage. But it has also produced the high degree of compartmentalization characteristic of present-day intellectual and occupational activity, and has brought about a technological revolution in the form and functioning of industrialized societies.

National and international air transportation is an impressive example. Clearly, extensive planning is required to create so large and complex a system of closely interrelated activity. Every aircraft is the product of decades of planning, research, development, and progressive improvement incorporating almost every field of knowledge and most areas of human endeavor. Safe and successful air operations require planning a worldwide system of airways, airfields, communication, personnel training, financial accounting, air traffic regulation, and operating procedures. An international network of communication and electronic computation provides immediate information concerning reservations, ticketing, and comparative airline scheduling. A particularly noteworthy achievement is the adoption of a common language for operational intercommunication among the more than a hundred and fifty nations and many languages involved in the far-flung air transportation system.

The structure of present-day industrial society has become so highly compartmentalized, complex, and sensitive that the inefficiency or failure of one part almost immediately affects another component, which in turn quickly influences other segments in a progressive chain reaction. Consider the disruption immediately brought about in a city by the failure of its electric power supply. Almost every aspect of urban life is affected: lights, electrically-powered water pumps, refrigerators, heating units, manufacturing machinery, and other equipment, radio and television. If power is not soon restored, prolonged use of emergency equipment powered by batteries becomes difficult or even impossible. The shock-wave of repercussions is progressively more extensive and intensive.

The intricate and sensitive organisms of modern industrial societies could not have evolved without the necessary capacity to plan. The successful fitting together of so many interdependent activities requires a high degree of conscious coordination and forethought. Since planning is necessary for the creation of complex organisms, it is also essential for their continued existence and progress. Breakdown of any one of its crucial components immediately disrupts the entire organism, and soon renders it inoperative.

Planning is required for the formation and continuation of every government, whatever its political, socioeconomic, religious, or cultural form. It is the objectives of planning, and the methods and extent of its application that differentiate political systems and ideologies. Autocratic governments apply it to achieve objectives imposed on the many by the few. Such regimes tend to become more rigid and destructive of freedom and individuality until they disintegrate because of their human invalidity, are overthrown by violence, or are successful in creating a population subservient to a ruling minority. Planning in democracies should represent the progressively enlightened will of an electorate. It makes possible that continuous progress toward individual and societal goals which is the mainspring of the democratic ethos, and it is a procedural means of synthesizing the contrasting forces comprising this political system.

There has been considerable debate concerning the political, social, and economic implications of planning a democracy (Finer, Hayek).* Although the meaningfulness of much of this discussion has been lost in a cloud of confusion between different kinds of planning which cannot be directly compared, there have been two underlying questions under scrutiny. What activities require or benefit from planning? Or conversely, what social mechanisms should be left to operate in a relatively spontaneous manner, without either supervisory limitations or deliberate incentives? And more specifically, for what activities and to what extent should the different levels of governmnet make plans?

Such debate is worthwhile because it promotes clarification of ends and means. But it neither denies the existence of planning in contemporary society, nor implies that human life is possible without planning in some form.

> We differ as to what and how much we plan, not whether or not we plan. . . . Those opposed to too much centralized planning do not suggest the alternative of aimless drifting with no plans at all. Certainly governments must make plans [like] individuals and businesses. . . . (Cordiner)

*References for Chapters One and Two are listed beginning on page 32. References for Chapter Three start on page 197.

The extent to which imprecise discussion of planning can confuse or misrepresent is worth emphasizing. The principal article in a stockholders publication of one of the largest corporations in the United States some years ago serves as a random but typical example. Its title "Planning Unplanned Research" was contradictory in itself, for research which is planned cannot also be unplanned. What was meant, of course, was research conducted with minimum predetermination, and maximum freedom to follow paths revealed during relatively undirected investigation. But not completely undirected, because undoubtedly the corporation would not have accepted research into subjects which could not conceivably relate to its current or future business. Some planning is necessarily involved in the conduct of any research. Both the title and the content of the article impute that planning should be avoided, whereas the actual claim is that a minimum of restrictive prior specification produces the best results in certain exploratory research.

In speaking of his early research, the author (an eminent scientist) reported that the

> . . . work wasn't planned. . . . It was allowed to grow by curiosity, by having fun. . . . it was because it wasn't planned that most of the successes resulted. . . . It seemed to me at the time . . . that planning is impossible. You can't plan to make discoveries. But you can plan work that will probably lead to discoveries.

The contradictions in this statement are self-evident. The deliberate avoidance of overplanning is itself a constructive planning decision. The fact that discoveries cannot be specifically planned, but an atmosphere can be created that is likely to lead to discoveries, suggests an optimum form of planning, not its exclusion. The unfortunate result of such careless or confused statement is the bias that it unintentionally or intentionally promotes against planning per se. This is unfortunate because the word is burdened with more than enough irrelevant associations and can so easily be used as a meaningless label or "glittering generality" (Lee). Careful use of terms is important because of the significance of planning in human affairs.

The future of humanity depends on planning—or the lack of it—more than any other activity. Merely feeding, clothing, and housing the population growth expected in most parts of the world during the next several generations will require extensive planning. Democratic societies in particular recognize the necessity of organized forethought to maintain the free political consensus which is their primary directive force, by strengthening existing procedures or developing new ones which contribute to its achievement. To this end, continuous evaluation of important changes in the structure of contemporary society is required. Political ideals and societal goals are rarely advanced by chance or neglect. Two examples of such changes underway today are the explosive growth of the mass media of communication which vitally affect hundreds of millions of people, and the growing difficulty or impossibility of the average voter comprehending the complex of considerations involved in most of the political decisions he makes.

The first of these changes is tying people together in a tight network of public and private intercommunication. Not so many years ago, word of mouth, personal mail, and the printed page were the principal means of communication. The volume of public information disseminated was but a tiny fraction of what it is today. And the time lag in this dissemination tended to cushion its emotional impact, and smooth immediate reactions into more extended and reflective reaction. Representative government was a geographical necessity because of the time involved in travel and communication to and from the seats of government.

Today, people are in almost instantaneous contact with each other, with all parts of the nation, and only to a slightly lesser extent with the world. Besides the rapid development of the older forms of communication made possible by expanding economies, high-speed printing presses, and rapid means of distribution, there is now the telegraph, teletype, radio, telephone, television, fiber optics, and orbiting satellite. And new means of communication are in the experimental stage. The actual and potential impacts of these media are enormous, for the number of people tied into the system and the volume of its output have vastly increased. Already, they have in effect quickened the pulse of the nation, because the dissemination of news is immediate and repetitive. National and international reactions and overreactions are simultaneously generated in hundreds of millions of people.

Increasingly, elected representatives and governmental appointees are tuned to the public opinion of the moment, rather than independently representative as conceived by the founding fathers. If present trends continue, it is conceivable that in time a system of direct voting by the public at large on proposed legislation may evolve. The body politic could follow legislative debate in the evenings on television and vote by push buttons built into the set. Votes would be automatically and immediately counted by electronic computers. The fact that this can be imagined confirms the reality of the changes which have taken place in mass communication, for it would have been almost inconceivable fifty years ago. A moment's reflection suggests the profound political and social consequences were direct legislative voting by the body politic to come about.

The potential moulding force of modern public communications is only now emerging. Information, misinformation, and conflicting material can be disseminated from relatively few centralized sources to many millions of people in an instant or within a few hours at the most. The possibilities of directed public opinion and mass public overreaction cannot be ignored because they are ideologically distasteful and raise thorny political problems. Today, the main motivation of the mass media of communication in the United States, is to attract, entertain, and influence people in a fiercely competitive business environment, rather than to enlighten, educate, and provide the balanced information and discussion required for the democratic political process to function most successfully.

Both general political issues and specific socioeconomic decisions become less and less distinct as industrialized societies become more complicated and compartmentalized. Scattered information and separate activities interrelate through a network of interconnection and chain reaction. Particular policies or programs may conflict without the voting public or their elected representatives being aware at the time of decision of the existence and consequences of contradictions. Or the cumulative outcome of separate actions may not be realized. For example, numerous benefits have been accorded military veterans over a period of many years: disability pensions, pensions to widows, bonus payments, special medical care, educational grants, special insurance, discounts on consumer purchases, use of certain military commissaries, preferential home loans, extra credits on civil service examinations and placement lists. All together, these provisions comprise a social policy of cumulative preferential treatment which is rarely recognized and considered in the aggregate.

Normally, the voter and legislator do not know how a decision expanding or contracting one activity will affect other established activities. There are only so many people, so many hours, and so much money available to a governmental entity at any given time. Unless these basic resources can be increased, additive and subtractive actions must be balanced. Even in areas of rapid population increase and an expanding economy, there is always a limit to the new services which can be financed from revenues derived from new sources of income. New or increased expenditures are not the result of deliberate choice between reducing, sustaining, or increasing existing activities, or providing new ones. Rather, expenditures are simply accumulated to meet voter demands until the exchequer or limits to increased debt force curtailment of some existing programs. Usually there is information concerning separate programs but insufficient analysis of them collectively. Maintaining an analytical representation or model which would include such a cumulative total presupposes the rational consideration and organized forethought characteristic of planning.

The adverse effects of irresponsible actions can accumulate to the point that it is difficult or even impossible to rectify the resulting situation when it is eventually recognized or acknowledged. Energies and resources are always wasted when mistaken decisions or activities persist through inadvertence or deliberate disregard. And the likelihood of undetected trends and potentially mistaken actions increases as societies become more complex. Since human knowledge is limited and many natural forces are unpredictable, the comprehensive planning process is formulated to reveal and accommodate unintended consequences before they become severely damaging.

It is a technical function of organized planning to maintain an integrated analysis of trends and specific developments within its area of concern, to anticipate the effects of inevitable change and thereby permit preventive or ameliorative action. In its portrayal of interrelationships between different elements and of events over time, this analysis reveals the repercussive and cumulative effects of isolated decisions. Thus, in the illustrative instance of veterans benefits, government officials and the body politic are better able to judge the desirability and feasibility of particular preferential treatment of this or any other special group if they are advised of the total benefits accorded over the years and the relationship of this commitment to other needs.

Although comprehensive planning provides the analytical reference required for more effective government, it does not decide if any action will be taken. This determination is made by the established mechanisms of political resolution in government, by executive decision in business, and by military command. The decision-maker may totally disagree with the planning analysis or arbitrarily reject it. But by supplying them with reliable information and analysis, planning supports the belief that providing decision-makers with better information and more complete analysis produces better decisions.

These contributions of planning are required by the expansion and compartmentalization of knowledge. There was a time when almost all of the information and analysis pertinent to a given situation could be comprehended by a single mind. Nowadays, highly specialized knowledge is needed to plan all but the simplest organisms. The correct decision may depend on interpretation of a legal technicality, the validity of a complicated engineering solution, the correct mathematical formulation of a computer program, or discovering the behavioral pattern of a hidden power structure. In each case, the decision-maker may need a specialist to provide the necessary information or judgment. Obtaining, evaluating, and coordinating these specialized inputs is one of the responsibilities of a comprehensive planning staff.

Evaluative techniques such as cost-benefit, cost-effective, and environmental impact analyses require more time than the usual decision-maker can spend on a single matter, unless it is a dire emergency. These important analyses are therefore usually conducted by the planning staff, in the manner generally prescribed by the decision-maker who will use them. Decision-makers must satisfy themselves that the many specialized inputs relevant to their conclusions are sound.

Self-sufficiency is no longer possible in technologically advanced societies because of the increased specialization of activities. Planning is required to integrate the multitude of separate but interdependent operations. Without it, current activities would cease functioning or a traumatic reversion to more primitive and self-sufficient conditions would have to occur. Few people and few organizations are self-sufficient today. Water, food, fuel, clothing, and the materials for shelter are produced by a few for the many. Especially in industrial societies the urban dweller is totally and immediately dependent on public utilities and private distribution systems and services of many kinds which supply the necessities for survival. Some seventy percent of the population of the United States, more than half of Europeans, and a growing percentage of people in developing countries live in cities. Without organized planning, modern urban activities and institutions could not exist in their present form.

As noted earlier, planning has been an essential aspect of human endeavor since earliest times. Certainly, the remarkable growth and development of the United States during its relatively short history could not have occurred without many forms of forethought. But the significance of comprehensive planning is not yet widely recognized. Its institutionalization as a directive and managerial activity in civil government has not yet been demonstrated in the United States. Unified planning by the four military services was introduced some thirty years ago, but is not yet fully realized in the command structure. The formation of corporate planning staffs by business is even more recent, but more widespread.

The trend of societies toward technological intricacy, economic sensitivity, and functional compartmentalization indicates that it is but a matter of time before comprehensive planning must be effected at national, state, and local levels of government. "Government by crisis" and "knee-jerk management," as they are sometimes called, are no longer feasible. Waste, confusion, and eventual breakdown are the inevitable result of reactive response rather than prescriptive planning. The consequences of inadequate comprehensive planning by governments in the United States today are found in the aggravated problems and generally unfavorable conditions within their respective jurisdictions.

Ultimate responsibility for the public welfare lies with government. In time, comprehensive planning will be established as an essential part of final decision-making by government. An analytical representation or "model" of actions, activities, and conditions within their respective jurisdictions will be maintained by federal, state, county, and muncipal governments. This informational and analytical statement of the best available knowledge concerning the past, present situation, trends, and interactions between major components of the organism will allow more accurate determination of the probable effects of different decisions before they are made. It will permit greater synthesis of constituent elements, produce greater constructive continuity over time. Data and analysis will be available to the different units of government, private enterprise, and the general public.

This analytical mechanism has been called the "institutional mind": considered by some so important to effective government that it should be established as the "fourth power" or fourth branch of government, co-equal with the traditional executive, legislative, and judicial branches (Tugwell).

This mind is independent of the personal minds of owners and managers, and of other individuals who may come and go, in whose collective activities the institutional mind expresses itself. This institutional mind has its powers of perception (investigation, research, experiment), or memory (records), or reasoning (analysis and comparison), and of design (planning and arrangement). Its life is coexistent with the life of the enterprise, and it can think and arrange affairs with that perspective made possible only by such characteristics. It has capacity to think in terms of experience larger than that which comes to any individual, to define distant goals, to arrange highly efficient ways and means of attaining them, and to pursue these distant ends consistently, yet with a flexibility which permits adjustment to changing conditions. (Taylor)

While the institutional mind has not yet been established in any government in the United States, it is developing within private enterprise. With the mounting complexity of business and the society of which it is part, and as businesses increase in size, chief executives are finding it next to impossible to maintain in their own minds a complete and up-to-date picture of the organization they direct and the environmental context within which it operates. The immediate demands upon the heads of companies of even moderate size have become so numerous and pressing that they do not have time to develop the facts and figures involved in many questions fundamental to the future of the enterprise. They are confronted with one urgent problem after another, each requiring their immediate personal attention until it is resolved. They carry a regular load of important policy, personnel, financial, and other managerial duties which they can never so completely delegate that they must not at least be regularly reviewed. Subordinate executives can provide information concerning their respective jurisdictions, and contribute judgments on those matters with which they are familiar. But the division or department head has neither the time nor the information to comprehend the company as a whole. Comprehensive corporate planning is the primary responsibility of the chief executive and the board of directors.

Although executive management makes many decisions from experience, there are many decisions—and they are usually the most critical—which require considerable preparatory investigation and technical research. Because of the pressure of immediate problems this work is often postponed until the value of anticipatory action is reduced and certain ways of solving the problem are no longer feasible. Even were the time available to chief executives to make their own studies, their time and abilities are more efficiently employed if background information, subordinate judgments, and preliminary analysis are provided for their further appraisal. If this analysis is carried a step further, in accordance with procedures they approve, their time can be concentrated on the conclusive choice between alternatives or the devising of a solution.

For these reasons corporate planning units have been established in many business organizations and are becoming more important in the conduct of the enterprise (*The Wall Street Journal*). Unlike planning performed by subordinate units, corporate planning is part of the office of the chief executive, as comprehensive planning by civil government is attached to the legislature or chief elected official. The corporate planning staff provides the chief executive of the business the background information and analysis he desires for his decision-making. Normally, this includes: operating data, current and projected into the future; forecasts for various time periods; and economic, political, social, and other analyses which relate to the company's plans for the future.

Corporate plans usually include the forthcoming budget year and the following year, which together constitute the short-range operating plan, and five additional years covering the medium-range future. Some elements of a business may be projected much further into the future. For example, tree farming by a wood products company may be planned and programmed for an eventual harvest thirty to sixty or more years in the future. Nowadays, it takes ten years or more to decide to proceed, plan, and construct most sizeable products and physical facilities such as a next generation computer, a new aircraft, power plant, or factory. Similarly, many policies and programs directed toward administrative-managerial change require extended periods of time for their realization.

Planning with more distant horizons had become a familiar theme among major American businesses, especially those competing in global markets. . . It is critical, executives say, to shift the rewards from quarter-to-quarter profit gains to the achievement of longer-term goals. (Hayes)

Every year or more often in emergency situations the planning staff analyzes the plans of subordinate units for the chief executive, and participates in their integration by top management into a comprehensive corporate plan for the enterprise as a whole. The information, analysis, and actions involved in this corporate planning over the years constitute the "institutional mind" of the company, continually used by successive chief executives to direct its "life" and future.

Even more than in civil government and business, planning is the essence of military activity. Since war determines whether a nation emerges as victor or vanquished, and military attack is usually conducted as a surprise, preparatory planning is clearly necessary. Also, emergency declarations in wartime permit immediate action and commandeering every human and material resource. The chain of command ensures positive organizational response by everyone involved. These characteristics and conditions of wartime favor total planning of military activity.

The extent of planning by the military is illustrated by the formal responsibility of the U.S. Joint Chiefs of Staff for strategic plans, joint logistic plans, integrated joint plans for military mobilization, combined plans for military action in conjunction with the armed forces of allies, and general policies and doctrines providing guidance in the preparation of detailed plans by other nations (*The New York Times*). Military systems require a high order of operational and project planning. The communications, logistics, and operations of some of these are global in scope: strategic bombing, intercontinental ballistic and cruise missiles, nuclear submarines, and various task forces.

Military planning is not intrinsically different from other planning. It has produced concepts and processes of general applicability: staff and line organization; remote sensing as a source of information; analysis by operations research teams; the systems approach; the process of planning, programming, and budgeting; and cost-effective evaluation.

Perhaps the most compelling forces for the further development and employment of planning are those arising from national needs, worldwide problems, and global crises. In the
United States, sooner or later, national land use, water conservation, air pollution, and transportation plans will be developed, formally adopted, and maintained. Disruption of the
ozone layer in the upper atmosphere and oil and pesticide pollution of the oceans require intercontinental planning, acid rain
and intracontinental water pollution international planning.
Powerful antagonisms and seemingly unreconcilable points of
view are straining international relations toward the nuclear
breaking point. For the first time in history, humans have the
capability to commit suicide as a species and bequeath the plan-
et to another animal. Resolution of this ominous state of existence will not occur by random chance, coincident awakening to
the danger, or fortuitous socio-political harmony. The only
realistic hope lies in deliberate planning and preventive action.

This does not suggest planning as a panacea. Planning is a
product of the human mind and spirit which achieves tangible
form only through human action. It is fundamentally a rational
process: thoughtful, inductive, analytical, and deliberate in nature. It requires the social ability and willingness to recognize
needs and problems, to relate cause and effect, to formulate objectives, and comprehend the probable future outcome of present and projected actions. It presupposes the emotional maturity to accept present restraints in favor of anticipated benefits at
some future time. The activity of planning requires in addition:
deliberate and effective organization, a reserve of human and
material resources which need not be used immediately but can
be withheld for future application, a minimum of relevant information, and superior analytical capabilities.

Although planning is properly categorized as a rational process, emotional factors are involved because it is a human concept and operates by human action. Inevitably, the technicians

and professional planners who formulate plans according to the objectives and general directives established by decision-makers are affected by their emotions as well as their rational minds. Because devising plans is creatively satisfying, their formulation is sometimes considered sufficient accomplishment in itself by those who conceive them, although they are operationally useless unless they are implemented: "a flower . . . born to blush unseen, And waste its sweetness on the desert air." In democratic societies, most plans are also subject to and affected by the emotional reactions of concerned individuals and special interest groups. Any conclusion that planning is exclusively rational is a misconception.

Were people consistently rational, their desires clear and consistent, and their emotional momentum always directed toward optimum collective goals, organized planning would maximize societal achievements. But not only does human behavior incorporate irrational emotional drives, but people are usually unaware of the extent to which unidentified and often irrelevant feelings affect what they believe is purely rational thinking.

Fluoridation of municipal water in the United States is an example. "No other public health measure has ever been so thoroughly studied and tested before it was introduced" (Mausner). Fluoride does not adversely affect the taste or quality of the water, and is very inexpensive. It would be hard to find a more desirable and relatively simple objective for rational planning. Yet efforts to fluoridate municipal water supplies have been voted down in a number of communities. Why?

> In short, the objections to fluoridation however unrealistic or unfounded, have deep psychological roots. . . . In contrast, the proponents of fluoridation have all too often ignored public psychology in presenting their case. . . . The greatest flaw has been the failure to prepare the public adequately. As a result there develops a polarization of attitudes which makes it very difficult to change opinion. (Mausner)

As occurred in this instance, planning programs may be identified with attitudes and issues which have little or no rational connection with the matter at hand but are considered very important and involve strong emotions. As often happens in human affairs, the program or issue becomes a vehicle of expression for pent-up feelings which do not really relate to the cause to which they have become attached. This is the usual tendency of some people, and the reaction of a majority in certain circumstances. Most people today would react to any reduction in the beneficial treatment of water rather than reject improving its quality. Emotional pendulums are capable of opposite extremes.

Plans that do not consider emotional factors and their effects may produce unexpected and unwanted results, if they are not rejected outright because of this vital omission. Emotional needs and attitudes, beliefs, customs, symbols, and other elements of individual and social psychology are as important considerations in planning as rational thought and processes. Plans are sometimes formulated by business that do not take into account predictable emotional reactions and behavior by unsympathetic employees or by a hostile executive whose cooperation is essential to success. Economic assistance to developing nations has been planned without regard to the educational level and occupational capability of the population, their beliefs, how they feel, think, and react. Any implicit assumption that most cultures are basically the same, or that the same plan will fit different cultural systems, usually results in failure, needless waste of money, unintended social dislocations, and missed opportunities to be helpful. It took years for the military to recognize the significance of "cold wars" which do not involve traditional weapons systems, strategy, and tactics. Nowadays it is recognized that the reactions, emotional attitudes, and minds of entire populations can be influenced through the mass media of communication. A war may be won before a conventional battle is fought.

Because emotional and behavioral factors are intangible and often transient, they are more difficult to calculate and incorporate in a quantitative plan than physical-spatial activities and facilities which can be more accurately measured. The rigorous quantitative statement and exact sequences of observable fact associated with science are possible only for those elements of comprehensive planning which permit this precision. Systematic understanding of socioeconomic, political, and psychological behavior cannot be developed with present knowledge because of the scope of necessary consideration and the many variables and intangibles involved.

The major problems of planning today spring from the fact that the behavioral maturity of people collectively has not kept pace with the tremendous scientific and technological advances of the past century. People will not cooperate sufficiently, or they do not choose to support the organized forethought that is not only possible but necessary for the effective functioning of many technical systems. On the international scene especially, emotional attitudes prevent effective planning to avoid nuclear war, global pollution, or widespread economic depression or social conflict. Whether passions or reason will prevail is the critical question of our time.

Myriad studies have been produced over the years relating to population, geographic conditions, economics, engineering, physical and social sciences, and many other subjects and fields involved in planning. In fact, all knowledge relates to comprehensive planning: at least in some indirect or remote way. But study of planning has not progressed beyond the initial descriptive stage. And study of the *general process and principles* of comprehensive planning per se has barely begun. Little has been produced concerning informational and analytical procedures and methods commonly employed in preparing, maintaining, and revising plans whether for business, government, or the military.

General principles are implicit in the application of every field of knowledge. They determine and give direction to important areas of procedural research. They clarify and define fundamental considerations which must be taken into account. But as yet no general principles have been formulated for comprehensive planning.

The various forms and applications of planning are legion, differing according to the nature and situation of the organism being planned and the objectives which are established. But the process of comprehensive planning is basically the same even in disparate situations. It is the common characteristics of this comprehensive planning process, however and whenever applied, which constitute its fundamental substance and support the formulation of general principles.

This should advance the capability of comprehensive planning to successfully shape human affairs by adding to basic knowledge of the process, thereby improving the education and performance in practice of professional planners. It should lead to "quantitative" laws and "deductive or axiomatic conclusions" which make comprehensive planning analysis more rigorous and accurate. Efforts to fill the gap in the literature of planning created by the absence of a general theory and principles may also stimulate creative thought and basic research concerning all aspects and applications of planning. Ultimately, this should benefit society.

> The structure and habits of democratic states . . . lack those elements of persistence and conviction which alone can give security. . . . Even in matters of self-preservation, no policy is pursued for even ten to fifteen years at a time. (Churchill)

> Failure to acquire the ability to exercise such foresight implies the danger of dissolution of the nation and disaster . . . the only debate worth any attention much longer

concerns the methods of organizing the necessary foresight. (Barnard)

References

Barnard, Chester I., (President, New Jersey Bell Telephone Company), *Methods and Limitations of Foresight in Modern Affairs,* Paper delivered at the Thirtieth Annual Convention of Life Insurance Presidents), New York, December 1936, pp. 1, 18.

Churchill, Winston S., *The Second World War, The Gathering Storm,* Boston (Houghton Mifflin), 1948, pp. 17, 18.

Cordiner, Ralph J. (President, General Electric Company), 1952, specific reference unknown.

Finer, Herman, *The Road to Freedom,* Boston (Little Brown) 1945, 228 pp.

Hayek, Fredrich A., *The Road to Serfdom,* Chicago (University of Chicago), 1944, 228 pp.

Hayes, Thomas C., "Managers Adopting Long-Term Outlook," *The New York Times,* 11 January 1981, XII p. 40.

Lee, Alfred McLung and Lee, Elizabeth Bryant (Editors), *The Fine Art of Propaganda,* New York (Harcourt Brace), 1939, pp. 47-68.

Mausner, Bernard and Judith, "A Study of the Anti-Scientific Attitude," *Scientific American,* Vol. 192, No. 24, February 1955, pp. 35-39.

The New York Times, 28 March 1948, p. 27.

Taylor, Fredrick W., specific reference unknown.

Tugwell, Rexford G., "The Fourth Power," *Planning and Civic Comment,* Part II, April-June 1939, 31 pp.; *The Emerging Constitution,* New York (Harper's), 1974, pp. 284-355.

The Wall Street Journal, Vol. CI, No. 104, 27 November, 1979, p. 1.

Three
GENERAL PRINCIPLES

Information n **1:** The communication or reception of knowledge or intelligence **2a:** knowledge obtained from investigation, study, or instruction **b:** INTELLIGENCE, NEWS **c:** FACTS, DATA **d:** a signal or character (as in a communication system or computer) representing data **e:** something (as a message, experimental data, or a picture) which justifies change in a construct (as a plan or theory) that represents physical or mental experience or another construct **f:** a quantitative measure of the content of information; *specif.* a numeral quantity that measures the uncertainty in the outcome of an experiment to be performed. . . .

(*Websters New Collegiate Dictionary*, Springfield, Massachusetts, 1973, p. 592)

INFORMATION
Collection and Utilization

INFORMATION IS OF COURSE, basic to all animate activity. Without information concerning the environment, biological organisms could not make the adaptations necessary for survival. Certainly, all human activities from their earliest beginnings have required descriptive information to comprehend the existing situation, and prescriptive information to determine actions to be taken.

Human information is derived through intuition, subjective judgment, and formal observation, examination, or survey. Intuitions are personal impressions or feelings acquired through sensory reactions unrecognized at the time. Subjective judgments are also personal and expressed in words, but they are

35

more deliberate and organized. They incorporate an undirected accumulation of observations and thoughts that may not be recalled specifically as a conscious sequence of cause and consequence. Most information employed in planning is the product of impersonal observation and organized survey: precise and numerical in its final form. The resultant data can be manipulated mathematically within the conceptual limits imposed by scientific method.

Since all three categories of information are involved in all comprehensive planning, their collection and utilization constitute its most basic principle. *Planning cannot be conducted successfully without information indicating the current state of the organism, its functioning as revealed by interrelationships between its primary elements, and trends that can be projected at least into the near future as a basis for conclusion and action.* All fifteen of the following principles in this book involve information in some derivative or integrally important way.

To illustrate. Allocation of resources (Principle 2) requires information to compare needs with available resources of people, time, and money. Planning for Peak Periods (Principle 13) occurs because of data disclosing the existence, frequency, magnitude, and duration of such periods. Feedback (Principle 10) is the correlation of information describing output with that describing input. Representation of the Entirety (Principle 8) is an informational mechanism pure but not simple. And if there were no intervals of relative stability in the continuous process of comprehensive planning, Resistance to Planning (Principle 16) would include reaction to the informational overload imposed on people in this way.

As would be expected, the form of the information used in comprehensive planning varies with the type of organism within which it is being applied, the kind and scope of the planning, and the goals and objectives selected. Business planning is conducted for the most part with monetary data depicting the operations and profitability of the enterprise. Military planning focuses on numbers of units in each of the elements in the long list of military personnel, weapons, and material: coupled with their respective lethality, vulnerability, and operational requirements under combat conditions. Although the monetary unit is not the primary quantification in military planning, cost determines the number of alternate systems which can be considered. Civil governmental planning employs numerical data for population, utilities, services, transportation, communication, income and expenditures, and other elements that can be measured and depicted in this way. It also maintains subjective information concerning the preferences, attitudes, and reactions of the public, political forces and legislative realities, and the explicit and implicit policies of the mass media of communication, financial and other power centers, and special interests affecting governmental planning.

The information needed for comprehensive planning is different at different administrative levels of the organism. Top management in business, military commanders, and ranking officials in civil government are more concerned with broader issues and considerations, overall problems and policies, than they are with specific operations which are planned and carried out at lower levels of the organization according to general directives decreed by higher authority. For example, multinational business planning requires such strategic information as the nature and extent of markets and competition abroad, or potential dangers to foreign investments of excessive governmental interference or eventual expropriation. Coalitions of hostile forces are a continuing concern of military planners, as are the predilections and intentions of legislators in civil governmental planning.

Pentagon Orders Upgrading of Military Data Gathering. . . . Among the changes in military strategy . . . has been the speed of response to what military planners call "ambiguous warning." The term refers to military alerts, troop movements, or other indications by potential adversaries in which the intent is not clear. (Halloran, 1982).

Operational planning, on the other hand, requires detailed information to plan and program the establishment of a business abroad, formulate specific war plans and tactics, or work out the exact language of a law and its implementing regulations.

Better information, assessment and transmission of intelligence data are needed for field commanders to consider and to speed up the response by American and allied forces. . . . (Halloran, 1982)

Precise data are needed for the short-range projections made in operations planning; and by definition "planning objectives" require sufficient detailed information to formulate the specific programs of implementation which they incorporate. However, long-range planning that is not strategic and "planning goals" involve a selection among analyses and scenarios of future development that are based on a much broader range of information than can be derived from the data employed in operations planning. As planning extends further into the future, the number and range of elements and uncertainties to be considered and the information needed for combined analyses accumulate at an increasing rate. And planning goals, which are "general desires or intentions, whose achievement is . . . hopeful, distant, and indefinite . . . cannot be formulated and programmed with sufficient specificity to be incorporated quantitatively in [a] comprehensive plan" (Chapter One).

Although the different organizational levels of planning and information within the organism are conducted separately, they are interdependent parts of one process. Faulty strategic planning cannot be corrected by superior planning at lower levels of effectuation. Poor or inconsistent operational planning can invalidate the best strategic planning. A significant change or circumstance at one level of an organism calls for revisions at other levels each of which maintains the information it needs to plan comprehensively for its area and scope of responsibility.

As discussed under Principle 8 (Representation of the Entirety), there is a core of most essential information for comprehensive planning which must be identified for each organism. The Open-End Context of Planning (Principle 7) presents an infinity of information that can be related logically to any comprehensive planning. Selection of the most critical data that the organism can afford to obtain and maintain is therefore necessary. For example, smaller businesses can be conducted with the data shown in Operating and Profit and Loss Statements and the Balance Sheet, although additional information would produce better planning. Comprehensive city planning can be effected with information concerning population, municipal income and expenditures, utilities and services, housing, land use, transportation, and political-legislative realities.

Within the core of most essential information, "key indicators" can be identified. Some of these represent matters of such paramount concern that they are continually monitored as part of comprehensive planning: for example, interest rates or sales-service levels in corporate planning. Some represent the collective state of a number of interrelated considerations: such as crime rates which reflect population characteristics, law enforcement, economic and social conditions. Others signify situations that can become serious problems or develop into a real and present danger: the percentage of the elements in a military system that are not "combat ready" or social conditions which could lead to civil disturbance.

Other things being equal, the broader the scope of comprehensive planning, the more diverse the information needed. Ordinarily, planning a business producing a single product or service is simpler than for one engaged in several different activities. Comprehensive planning for combined military operations is more demanding and requires more information than planning for a smaller unit. And almost by definition, planning for the full range of civil governmental responsibilities is far more complex and requires much more information than planning comprehensively for a single municipal function such as police or fire protection.

The reliability of the information used in planning—and in every other human activity—is clearly vital. Because certain data are highly touted and widely used does not signify that they are accurate. An outstanding example of numerical misinformation, ingrained in the minds of many people by yearly repetition and unquestioning acceptance, are the statistical reports on the number of deaths by automobile accident in the United States during holiday weekends. Yearly increases in the number of these deaths are cited as evidence of increasing hazard, whereas in actuality the increasing *safety* of automobile travel is shown by the decreasing number of deaths per mile traveled by car. Another example is the continuing debate over whether the number of crimes is increasing or a larger percentage of them are being reported. The reliability of data is indicated not only by whether they measure what they purport to, but also by their plus-or-minus percentage of significance or accuracy: a figure rarely included with the publication of or presentation of numerical information.

Careful interpretation and use of data counteract the natural tendency to ascribe greater validity to statistics than to other forms of information, simply because numbers by their nature suggest greater precision. Economic prediction demonstrates the need for informational skepticism. Despite the multitude of relevant numerical data available and the significance of economic conditions for most human activities, economic forecasting is notoriously unreliable: both with respect to general economic conditions and particular elements such as interest, unemployment, and inflation rates, price levels, and the stock market. Reliability is necessarily a continuing concern of comprehensive planning. To the extent possible, it is better to use

fewer data of higher reliability than a larger number of less accurate data. In this way not only are the data more accurate in
themselves, but their separate percentage inaccuracies are less
likely to be compounded into even greater errors when the different elements are combined in comprehensive planning analysis.

Related to reliability is the meaningfulness of information.
The meaningful conclusions that can be drawn from a random
opinion survey are limited compared to those that can be derived from the scientifically structured sample survey which produces results with a calculable percentage accuracy. A mathematically defined random sample, on the other hand, is most
meaningful for the quality control of manufactured products.
Simply comparing the numbers of military weapons does not
take into account their respective lethality, vulnerability, or
combat readiness; and comparing the services provided by different local governments is misleading if there are appreciable differences in what they include. The significance of debt for a
business is not only its amount, but its relation to liquid assets,
record of profitability, product share of the market, and the interest rate and maturity date of the debt.

Continued use of data that have been collected every year to
reveal "vertical" trends over time is precluded if the collection
or content of the data is altered sufficiently to render them no
longer statistically comparable. Sometimes they can be statistically adjusted at added cost and time to maintain comparability.
Similarly, the "horizontal" comparison of different elements of
an organism at any one point in time requires their expression in
units that can be correlated mathematically. Monetary data
describing one element of an organism cannot be mathematically integrated with non-monetary quantities or with subjective
information in some estimated order or weighting, unless a
meaningful method of conversion or a common denominator of
comparison is devised. It is, of course, the old story of adding
apples and pears.

Information needed for comprehensive planning that is not maintained within or outside the organism can usually be obtained at a cost. Of course, when data maintained elsewhere for other purposes can be used, the cost of comprehensive planning is reduced accordingly. Determining what information to acquire from within and from outside the organism, what to collect *de novo,* and what to maintain regularly with the funds available is a crucial and continuing decision. The costs attributable to the central comprehensive planning unit of an organism are reduced when part of the information needed is gathered by and charged to decentralized components; but the cost of analytically integrating the information provided by the different decentralized activities for top management remains approximately the same.

Insofar as one can generalize, censuses, remote sensing, and sample surveys are superior sources of information. Together, they provide an adequate informational base for much comprehensive planning. Censuses supply the most complete and accurate data concerning population, housing, and other facts about people that can be obtained in no other way. Remote sensing produces the largest quantity and most diverse information from any single source, at affordable cost. Aerial photographic interpretation provides the wealth of cartographic, physiographic, geographic, geologic, and other information that can be seen and analyzed from an overhead view. It reveals the location and size of almost all structures, vegetation, land uses, and human activities on the ground. Additional more specialized information can be obtained: such as agricultural crop forecasts, the extent of certain plant disease infestation, concentrations of fish underwater, or underground thermal energy sources and archaeological ruins. Remote sensing is a particularly valuable source of information for developing countries that have not established an informational base and are undertaking comprehensive planning for the first time. Remote sensing is also an important means for gathering military intelligence and monitoring the observance of disarmament treaties. Sample surveys are widely recognized as the best or only method of determining people's attitudes and specific opinions at affordable cost, collecting information that can be reliably sampled, and simplifying certain mathematical analyses.

The modern industrialized world is producing enormous quantities of information through explosive expansion of the mass media of communication, widespread fact-gathering by the growing number of institutions and organizations of all kinds, and the storage and immediate availability of more and more computerized data. There is every prospect that this rapid growth will continue unabated. By contrast, analytical capabilities of digesting, integrating, and drawing sound conclusions from this mass of information have nowhere near kept pace. As a consequence, there is real danger of informational constipation, of intellectually drowning in the flood of readily available data that cannot now be effectively assimilated and analyzed. And people's capacity to act wisely in their own collective best interest appears to advance little or not at all. Comprehensive planning must restrict its conclusions to what can be evaluated and analyzed, and its recommendations to what decision-makers want or may be induced to accept.

In this connection, it is known that graphical portrayal is the most widely comprehended form of presenting information. Mathematical constructs are intelligible only to those disposed toward abstractions and those who have learned the language of mathematics. Because it is still true that "a picture is worth a thousand words," graphical expression is usually the best way of making most information intelligible to the largest number of people. Comprehensive planning is self-defeating if it is explained and presented in ways that are difficult for both decision-makers and its larger constituency to comprehend, or if understanding the information requires undue effort on their part.

Allocation. . . .
1. Act of putting one thing to another; a placing; arrangement.
2. Allotment or apportionment. . . .

Resources. . . .
2. pl. Specif.: Available means, as of a country or business; computable wealth in money, property, products, etc.; immediate and possible sources of revenue. . . .

(*Webster's New International Dictionary of the English Language,* Second Edition (Unabridged), 1960, Vol I, p. 69; Vol. II, p. 2122).

AVAILABLE RESOURCES
Allocation

THERE IS ONLY SO much energy in the world at any given moment; and there are only so many resources available for comprehensive planning at any particular time. Human, financial, and material resources and time are required. How many people with what skills, special knowledge, or general capability are needed and how many are available? How much additional money can be obtained or what re-allocation of current resources can be made without curtailing or eliminating some activities to the detriment of the organism as a whole? What existing material resources can be used most advantageously to what ends, reducing the need for new acquisitions? How much time can be spent before a decision must be

made, or the results of the planned effort must be realized if it is
to serve its purpose? Every societal organism must determine
what resources are available to it and how they are employed. If
this is not done consciously and deliberately, it is implicit in the
actions that are taken or in whatever activities occur.

When crisis conditions exist everything is devoted to resolv-
ing the emergency situation. If all available resources are needed
to maintain current operations, none are at hand for anything
else. An organism can find the wherewithal for improvements
or new developments if it determines that the resources available
to it are not being used effectively, and therefore all of them are
not needed to maintain current activities. If discretionary resources are not available by increasing internal efficiency, the
organism must acquire additional resources for the planning
purpose from outside.

The different components within human organizations vie
with each other for a share of the total resources available. Each
seeks a substantial if not major share for itself. This form of internal organizational competition is well-known, widely practiced, and considered constructive or inevitable in some societies. Subordinate executives together ask for more resources
than are available to the organism as a whole. Normally they do
not know what other units are requesting. In part they hold
their managerial positions because they are ambitious for themselves and their units. Also their personal success depends on
whether they achieve the objectives set for them by higher authority or those they set for themselves; the accomplishments of
their units are compared with those of similar components of
the same or comparable organisms. This competition is considered a constructive effort on the part of unit managers to advance the activities, attainments, and prospects of their division
or department for the benefit of everyone concerned. Whether
or not such competition is encouraged as it is in the United
States, it is present in one way or another in most societies be-

cause of people's inherent and inevitable self-interest and consequent rivalry with others.

Top managers—whether elected representatives, other government officials, business executives, or military commanders —know that they cannot fully satisfy the requests of subordinate units which always add up to more capital, facilities, personnel, or other support than the parent organization can provide. There are never enough resources to fulfill all requests, needs, demands, or ambitions. For these reasons *the most essential function of comprehensive planning is the allocation of available resources among competing needs.*

Not only must this be done to optimize the achievement of the organism and its constituent parts, but it is an operational necessity. Productive activities simply do not function unless there is at least a minimum degree of intentional or fortuitous allocation of available resources among the elements of the productive process. In comprehensive planning this allocation is made for the current planning period (normally a year), for the shorter-range operational future (from three to seven years depending on the nature of the organism and activity), and often much further into the future for certain activities.

Allocating resources over time requires: identification and integration of Primary Elements; their Projection into the future; balancing Natural, Human, and Purposive Change; consideration of Uncertainty, Risk, and Ambiguity; and other general principles of comprehensive planning covered in this book. The informational-analytical mechanism employed to do this is the Representation of the Entirety explained and discussed in a subsequent section. Viewed in this way, the remaining principles of comprehensive planning support its basic function of allocating available resources.

Of course, this allocation could be done by personal subjective judgment with little or no help from organized informational and analytical procedures: "seat of the pants" management as it was first called in the aircraft industry. But organized planning has become so essential a directive activity in today's world—with every indication that it will be even more so in the world of tomorrow—that a predominantly intuitive approach no longer suffices. This accounts for the great increase during the past twenty-five years in the number of city managers, corporate planning staffs, expanded planning activities within the military services, and the establishment of the U.S. Congressional Budget Office.

Identifying and assigning resources are made more difficult by the fact that they vary in type and amount over time: depending on the internal operating condition of the organism, plans and commitments for its future, and the external environment which is likely to limit its prospects or favor certain planning objectives. If current operations are not going well, resources intended for another purpose may be needed to correct this situation. Military requirements and plans change with new treaties, defense commitments, and observed shifts in the intentions, weaponry, strategy, and activities of potential adversaries. The scope of civil governmental planning has been expanded by greater awareness of pollution culminating in pioneering national and state environmental legislation enacted in the early 1970s.

New technology can alter the resources required for an activity or product. For example, the size, cost, and marketing of electronic computers have been significantly changed during the past decade by the increased capacity and reduced cost of microchips, brought about by technological advances in their design and manufacture. Comprehensive planning by the military services has been greatly affected by developments since the close of World War II in the size and power of explosive devices, the accuracy with which they can be guided to targets, means of propulsion, and almost every component of combat: aircraft, missiles, nuclear submarines, tanks, and other military weapon systems. Improvements in mobile communications and medical diagnostic and resuscitator equipment have made possible paramedical emergency service in cities. In each of these examples technological advances have required a re-allocation of available resources by the responsible organism: with respect to budget commitments, personnel requirements and training, material procurement and supply, and other elements of comprehensive planning.

The resources available to an organism at any given time vary with how much it can plan for the future. If policies or circumstances prevent assigning resources to planning objectives whose benefits will not be realized until some future time, more resources are available for current allocation. The attitudes of executive decision-makers, customers, stockholders, and the body politic vary considerably concerning how much of currently available resources should be withheld from present use and directed toward results that are planned for some future time and are therefore less certain. People's reluctance to sacrifice today for the future is discussed in the final section of this book on Resistance to Planning: Inevitable Reality.

The nature and relative availability of human, financial, and material resources also vary with the stage of socioeconomic development of the organism. As would be expected, the educational level and professional characteristics of the human resources available in developing and developed countries are very different. And developing countries do not have the wherewithal nor have they had the time to produce the level of material goods and physical facilities found in countries with longer histories of modern economic development. The capability to accumulate financial capital and to apply new technology also depends on the stage of development of the country. Similarly, the material resouces available to newly founded business enterprises and military services are different from those that are well established. The time ordinarily required to achieve planning objectives is not necessarily longer in developing countries, depending on whether those objectives take advantage or run counter to the social, economic, or cultural usages of the country.

Since directly and indirectly politics pervades all activity, politicians are a vital part of a societal endeavor as all-encompassing as comprehensive planning by civil government. Ordinarily, staff conclusions reached by purely rational review and analysis must be modified to fit the less rational world of political decision-makers who represent the public will and reflect public irrationality in democratic governments, and determine what the public must accept in autocratic regimes. With immediate mass communication and frequent polls of people's attitudes, desires, and reactions, public opinion and the pressures applied by numerous special interests shape civil governmental planning in the United States: influencing or directly determining the political conclusions of elected representatives and the legislation they enact. Comprehensive planning maintains analytical information not only on the functioning of the political process, but also on the opinions and desires of those for whom it is conducted. If some of these opinions and desires are sufficiently strong and permanent, the planning staff may be obliged in good conscience to incorporate them in its recommendations even if it is doubtful that they will be accepted by those who make the comprehensive planning decisions.

Public politics also affect comprehensive planning by business and the military. The news media in the United States carry stories almost daily concerning the impact of government regulations and decisions on business. Proposed weapon systems and the conduct of the military services are subject to congressional review and approval. Of course, the nature and extent of political influence on business and military planning vary with different government systems. But in one way or another, politics is always a powerful directive force because it signifies what is societally desirable, feasible, or acceptable. And it indicates how a proposed comprehensive plan can best be guided through the process of political acceptance.

What can be called internal or private politics also affects comprehensive planning of all kinds. In addition to the usual competition among organizational units referred to above, there are the personal politics involved in pursuing purely selfish self-interests. Either or both of these forms of internal politics may be found among the staff responsible for comprehensive planning recommendations as well as among those in the units it integrates.

Since politics is society's primary directive force and main means of expression, its determinative effects on the allocation of available resources in comprehensive civil governmental planning represents society's conclusions concerning its present and future, and the extent to which it is willing to engage in such overall planning. Less direct but almost equally impactful are the effects of politics on business and military planning.

Ordinarily, success enhances available resources by attracting the best people, raising the general level of confidence and morale, increasing the ability of the organization to borrow money or secure additional public support or a larger share of tax revenues, and by other favorable consequences that result from a record of achievement.

The successful allocation of available resources in comprehensive planning also depends on the integrated scheduling of the times programmed for the attainment of each planning objective separately. As indicated under Explanation of Essential Terms on page 5, the statement of every planning objective incorporates the resources and program of actions required for its effectuation. Invariably, there are certain interrelationships between different planning objectives which determine the optimum sequence for their separate and integrated implementation. Changes in a carefully integrated program of implementation that prevent one program from correlating effectively with another can cause a re-allocation of the resources available.

A form of resource allocation also occurs in animate entities which do not include people. Biological organisms exhibit a progressively more effective distribution of activity among their respective parts during the evolutionary process, responsive to changes in the external environment. Mutations constitute especially significant rearrangements of parts. When injured, the components of biological organisms react in different combinational ways to heal the wound or compensate for the damage done. Inanimate organisms also re-allocate their components when adjusting to different conditions: metallic rust as a reaction to moisture, ashes as a reconstruction of matter brought about by fire, or the change of one chemical compound into another. These are resource re-allocations in a particular sense of the words.

Change. . . .
1. A succession or substitution of one thing in the place of another; alteration of conditions or circumstances. . . .
2. Any variation or alteration; a passing from one state or form to another. . . .

(*Webster's New International Dictionary of the English Language,* Second Edition (Unabridged), 1960, Vol. I, p. 449)

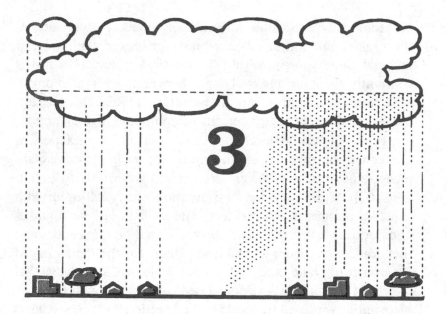

NATURAL, HUMAN, AND PURPOSIVE CHANGE

Interrelationships

Natural Change

NATURAL CHANGES ARE THE result of forces of nature over which humans have little or no control, individually and collectively. This absence of control may be absolute because there is no conceivable way people can significantly influence the natural force: for example worldwide ocean tides, the direction of the Gulf Stream, or the monsoons. It may be a practical lack of control because the resources required to modify the natural situation are excessive. Or the personal and social restraints required to modify the natural change are technically impossible or politically unacceptable: such as the total elimination of soil erosion or the immediate halting of national population growth. The physical-biological world is constantly changing and evolving. There are only limited or relative states of equilibria and no universal climax. This fact underlies many necessary provisions of comprehensive planning.

At the molecular level, the expansion and contraction of matter are natural changes taken into account in planning man-made structures; coefficients are derived from tests to permit prediction of the variation of dimension which will occur with expected changes in temperature. The incidence of earthquakes and floods is reflected in local governmental building codes and the location or design of buildings. Plans for the replanting of cut-over forest land take into account ecological knowledge that in certain geographical regions one type of plant will predominate initially, providing shade and protection for tree seedlings which in time will become dominant. Animal life will change symbiotically with successive botanical stages as the natural environment develops toward a period of climactic equilibrium.

Plans relating directly to people collectively are drawn in terms of current trends and anticipated changes in the size, composition, and age of the population: social security and private pension plans, production plans for many consumer goods and services, or policies and plans involving a political constituency. People are so much of the essence in most plans that inevitable changes in their characteristics and behavior must be taken into account. Of course, populations are also affected by purposive changes incorporated in a wide variety of policies and programs relating to birth control, income, taxes, medical care, social security, and religion.

Before phenomena of natural change can be considered in planning, an observed pattern in their occurrence or a sequence of cause and effect must permit a degree of reliable prediction. And their effect on the organism involved must be sufficiently understood to allow a deduction of consequences. This is relatively easy for the simpler phenomena for which conclusive data have been developed, such as the change in the dimensions of materials noted under Tolerance and Flexibility, Principle 12. But there are many activities and events important for comprehensive planning for which reliable data are not available, even in industrialized countries: data depicting the interactions among major urban components needed for sound city plans; information concerning research and development by business competitors needed for corporate plans; or adequate intelligence concerning foreign countries and their military capabilities required for war plans. In developing countries there are often serious informational inadequacies affecting planning. And there are, of course, numerous natural changes among the multiple phenomena and complex interactions of large-scale ecological and environmental systems which are simply not yet sufficiently understood to be incorporated in comprehensive planning.

Ordinarily, natural changes are first identified and understood within a particular intellectual discipline or field of endeavor. Mutation was first noted in biology, and its most intensive study, systemization, and utilization have been in this field. The periodicities of stellar bodies are associated with astronomy, or radioactive decay with chemistry. These natural changes are first taken into account in planning within the respective field. As their interrelationships with other phenomena are established, they are considered in a wider range of planning. The periodicity of the moon and its relationship to tides is taken into account indirectly in plans for coastline facilities and development, and in military plans for amphibious operations. The cycle of sun spot intensification, originally only of theoretical interest to astrophysicists, is now a factor in radio communications planning because of its relationship to atmospheric noise disturbance.

Some natural changes are relevant to most planning because of their universality in different forms: climatic variations, time, expansion and contraction, deterioration. The significance of natural change for planning varies with the type of organism and its situation. In agricultural planning, climatic change is crucial. In planning a company's advertising campaign, the significance of natural change is normally much less. Expansion and contraction of physical materials are very different from expansion and contraction of a city or social institution, although both are variations in size over time resulting from an imbalance of internal and external forces. There are also great differences in the extent of knowledge concerning these phenomena in different contexts. The causes and effects of dimensional changes in most materials are well established and incorporated in hundreds of thousands of engineering designs. But the implications for environmental planning of the cyclical expansion and contraction of diverse ecological components are only partially understood. For a long time, the deterioration of physical plant has been taken into account in business planning by amortization, but the importance for health planning of understanding the particular economic, social, and medical problems of people as they grow old and deteriorate physiologically and psychologically has only recently been recognized in the United States.

Many natural changes are influenced by people. Cloud seeding and nuclear energy have opened up new possibilities of manipulating atmospheric forces recently considered beyond human intervention. But manipulating the weather introduces new economic, legal, and political questions of artificially favoring one region by depriving another. Human populations can be altered by nutrition, birth control, abortion, and in time genetic engineering. Humans are engaged in a never-ending battle to control the natural change of rodent, insect, and bacteriological populations. They seek to arrest the decline of species in danger of extinction, to create genetically improved animals for the commercial market.

Human actions are in constant interplay with natural forces. The denuding of forest land for timber drastically alters the microenvironment and greatly increases soil erosion, setting in motion the ecological succession previously mentioned. The long-range effects on the natural environment and on human reproduction of powerful insecticides, radioactive nuclear waste, nuclear explosions, and industrial air pollution are not yet known specifically. Natural changes created or altered by people which have already occurred cannot be cancelled: only modified or possibly reversed. Some alteration of natural conditions, such as the increase of carbon dioxide and ozone levels in the upper atmosphere caused by human activities, can never be modified or eliminated: only countered conceivably at some future time.

Most natural changes can be altered at least to some small degree by human activities. But as it is always the case, the feasible application and extent of every human activity depends on the resources of people, time, energy, and money available for the effort. In the ultimate sense, people are forever subject to natural changes since they can hardly redirect the universe. There are natural changes to which they must adjust as best they can, those they could affect were the required resources available, and those within their capabilities which they decide to modify. All of them should be taken into account in planning.

The rate at which a natural change occurs is an important consideration in planning. If it is gradual—such as a change in the long-range weather pattern, the birth rate, or most ground movement—there is usually time to "wait and see," to observe, confirm the trend, and establish its characteristics more exactly before acting. Any required reformulation of existing plans can be correspondingly gradual, with less disruption of programs in process and easier redirection of effort toward new or revised planning objectives.

Natural changes that occur at a rapid rate are ordinarily more impactful, both individually and conjointly, than those which change slowly; they call for more immediate reaction in planning. Thus, a change in the incidence of a particular disease may require corresponding change in a health plan. Or an increase in soil erosion and flooding caused by precipitation above the maximum recorded historically may call for immediate readjustment of allowable densities of development in urban planning, or changes in corporate business or project plans which involve use of the land subject to unexpected erosion and flooding. An attentive eye on pertinent natural changes is part of the continuous process of comprehensive planning. A striking example is the Netherlands which has reclaimed most of its land area from the sea, and must keep a close and constant watch on its coastline and protective dikes to ensure that some weakening does not develop and threaten to inundate large sections of the country.

There are also, of course, the natural changes of an institutional nature which apply to planning itself as well as to the organisms with which it is concerned. Institutions exhibit an evolutionary sequence of development comparable to that which characterizes the life of individuals: birth, youth, maturity, impaired capability, eventual disintegration, and death. Fortunately for comprehensive planning, institutions have longer life spans than individuals because the regular replacement of personnel normally prolongs the organizational cycle of initiation, operation, and eventual dissolution. Even early bureaucratic disintegration does not necessarily lead to immediate organizational death. Because planning is the most important process in an organization, normally conducted by its top management, it must continually seek to stretch out the cycle of growth and decline which is typical of institutions as well as individuals.

Planning can guard against natural deteriorative change within itself by employing methods which have proven generally successful: periodic management review by an outside group of qualified people; self-appraisal including comparing planning proposals with their results; frequent advisory contact with authorities in the fields most crucial in the planning process; administrative organization and procedures designed to promote intercommunication and managerial advancement; encouragement of in-service training and continuing education.

At times it may be necessary to make the best possible assumption or even best guess concerning natural change, if the formulation of the plan requires it. During the Second World War, many assumptions were necessary concerning the geographical characteristics of islands in the Pacific which were to be invaded; reliable up-to-date information was not available from the usual sources. Fortunately, much of the information needed for successful amphibious landing and military occupation could be derived from aerial photographic interpretation: tidal range, offshore currents, underwater obstructions, topography, ground cover, and soil conditions. And on the assumption that this photographic information was not totally reliable, invasion plans were drawn with sufficient flexibility to allow for contingencies.

In general, *natural changes establish the potentialities and limitations of the external environment within which comprehensive planning operates.* To alter them is usually impossible; to compensate for the difficulties they may impose requires time, energy, and money. Whether this use of resources is worthwhile to incorporate in plans is an important decision. An example in corporate business planning is whether to air-condition physical facilities for a few hot summer months. How important is controlled temperature and humidity to labor productivity and morale, to the efficient functioning of automatic machines, electronic computers, or robots? How much difference in environmental conditions between the inside and outside of buildings increases absenteeism from colds and other respiratory ailments? Are microclimatic measures such as increased insulation, natural air circulation, cool colors in the workplace, and more frequent rest periods—requiring much less capital investment—preferable in the long run because the capital resources saved in this way can be applied elsewhere in the company? Is air-conditioning a worthwhile investment in case of unanticipated sale of the facility sometime in the future?

Another illustration, regional in scope, of the relationship between the natural environment and comprehensive planning is:

> governmental planning for operation of the dams in the vast Missouri Valley project. . . . Here are two groups of interdependent factors: (1) the ever-changing, sometimes freakish, conditions of the river and its watershed, and (2) the man-made conditions that result from the operation of the chain of dams. The objective: to control the dam spillways and gates to get the greatest benefit in power, irrigation, and flood protection—three interests that often compete with each other. . . . Operation of the river and its dams. . . . can be important in more ways than one. For example, if dams and water level can be controlled even 1% more efficiently, the whole project can gain $500,000 in salable electric power. (*Business Week*)

Natural change is represented in this illustration by the physical behavior of the river, determined by conditions in its watershed and geographically related area which it is impossible or impractical to control. Man-made dams, power plants, and irrigation and flood control systems have not only changed the previous hydrological conditions, but they permit human-directed changes in the level and quantities of water stored behind the dams, the formation of new reservoirs, and varying rates of flow of water and the amount of silting. And, of course, man-made roads and structures have altered the environment in other ways.

Human Change

Basic to planning in every way is people's capability to affect by their own actions themselves, their environment, and their future. In so doing, they necessarily affect the future of humankind. This capability of purposive change is the raison d'être for planning and its most fundamental characteristic. Consideration of ends, goals, or objectives for any human action signifies a desire and intent to bring about change. Change induced and directed by humans is implicit in the definition of planning.

Each act of everyday planning by the individual is intended to produce some change, be it the meal prepared or the telephone call completed. All military planning seeks to achieve strategic and tactical superiority over potential adversaries or to win the war in active conflict. Optimization of profit and business survival are the ultimate objectives of the human changes comprising corporate planning. The general public welfare or a particular condition of the population in autocratic societies is the ultimate purpose of the human changes specified in civil governmental planning by city, county, region, state, and nation.

The extent of human change is determined by the total current and projected resources available to the organism. Whatever attainments are desired, only those intentional changes are possible that do not exceed the human and material capacity of the organism to effectuate. And since desirable advancements normally exceed the capacity of organisms to achieve them, the selection and implementation of human change is always a matter of choice, and invariably a compromise between what is wanted and what is possible. Planning provides the continuous background of information, special knowledge, analysis, and judgment needed by those who make this selective decision.

Many factors determine the choice and priority of purposive change desired by different societal groups and organizations. In one culture, material progress in productive plant, goods, or services may be paramount. In another culture with different values, less tangible advancements of an attitudinal or spiritual nature may be paramount. Certainly, the history, contemporary situation, direction of development, and external environment of every organism determine the nature of the purposive changes sought at any particular time. Purposive changes shift as internal and external conditions vary. For some organisms, allocation of total capability into many small incremental advances is desired, while for others greater achievement along but several lines is preferable. In some situations, realization in the near future is wanted, while at other times purposeful progress is measured according to a longer-range concept of time.

The selection of purposive human changes is also influenced by the availability of operating mechanisms to put them into effect. Having to establish new institutions to attain a particular objective will not only postpone its realization, but could cause its abandonment in favor of another objective for which organizational means of implementation already exist. At the higher levels of executive direction, purposive changes are formulated as general policies, at the lower administrative levels programmatic specificity is necessary.

Determination of what people want is never easy. It is especially difficult in the case of civil governmental plans that seek to optimize the general welfare. Not only must current desires be ascertained, but their relative intensity must be gauged. Are these desires fleeting? Are they long-range objectives in themselves, or temporary wants reflecting more fundamental and continuing goals? Some projection of wants into the future is required, so that insofar as possible longer-range planning programs will be in accord with the desires which prevail at the time of their completion. It is a responsibility of the representative political process to present the voter with the probable outcome of his choice among purposive goals; planning contributes the technical analysis required to develop this composite projection.

Human change involves fundamental desires: for food, clothing, and shelter, physical security, avoidance of risk, material possessions, opportunity to be heard by government, justice, freedom to travel. Such desires are strong forces which cannot be ignored in successful planning. Their identification is a foremost goal of the political process in democratic societies. They will vary with different cultures and conditions. Material wants increase with wealth. Spiritual needs are preeminent in cultures dominated by religion. And increasingly the mass media of communication determine the priority of wants and create new desires for many people.

Better understanding of people collectively can be expected in the future: their basic emotional drives and needs, temporary reactions, deep-rooted and more permanent responses. In business it is now recognized that a working atmosphere of acceptance, appreciation, and sympathetic contact can be as important to employee contentment and productivity as appreciable differences in remuneration. In military planning, the significance of psychological motivation and morale is acknowledged together with the importance of immediate response to command.

As psychological understanding expands, people will acquire greater understanding of their own emotions. Not only does this affect their personal contentment and relationship with others, but it contributes to the success of democratic planning. It promotes recognition of momentary overreactions which are natural and inevitable and must therefore be taken into account in comprehensive planning, but are not a sound basis for the selection of longer-range goals and objectives. Thus, emergency drills are partly for the purpose of countering the panicky reaction which can be expected if the exercise of more rational and constructive response is not planned and practiced. To the extent people identify unconstructive emotionality, the course of comprehensive planning is not continually diverted to run before the shifting winds of momentary overreaction, and there is less likelihood of planning which psychologically manipulates the public without their awareness. And individual decision-making in planning is improved to the extent unconstructive personal overreactions are minimized.

Purposive Change

By definition, the word change connotes consequences or results: consciously purposeful when introduced and directed by humans; evolutionally purposeful or serving a useful function in the case of most natural changes; and without determinate purpose but with identifiable consequences in the case of some natural phenomena.

The primary measure of achievement for any human organism is its capacity to adopt realistic goals, to formulate and effectuate planning objectives which advance the organism toward these goals, and to modify goals and objectives as attitudes and conditions change. Since purposive change in the general public interest is the fundamental intent of democratic societies, the ends and means of the planning process must reflect the collective desires and decisions of the body politic. This is not the responsibility of staff planning but of the elected and appointed decision-makers to whom it is advisory in representative governments, or the ruling powers in dictatorial regimes.

Both natural and human changes are purposive in different ways. Evolution is genetically directed toward advancing the capability of a species to survive. Biological organisms interact within their natural environment to attain and maintain climactic equilibrium. Even earthquakes serve to relieve geological pressures that have built up within the earth. Other natural changes produce cumulative effects which do not appear to serve a demonstrably useful function: soil erosion operating relentlessly to reduce land surfaces ultimately to the level of the oceans, hurricanes, or tsunami waves.

Most natural changes involve forces which have evolved over millions of years. The more man learns about them, the more he realizes their tremendous complexity, subtlety, and sensitivity, and how little is known concerning their functioning. When natural forces are considered collectively, man's comprehension of their myriad interactions and operation as an organismic whole is very limited.

Without adequate knowledge it is inadvisable to interfere with natural systems of change and interaction more than is necessary or clearly desirable. The extent to which the consequences of intervention in natural processes cannot be foreseen is illustrated by the unanticipated ecological effects of DDT, the vulnerability to decimating disease of genetic strains of grain developed exclusively for maximum yield, the unexpected birth defects caused by medicinal use of thalidomide, or the unforeseen destructive effects on the environment of unrestricted strip mining. With recent advances in nuclear physics, genetic biology, chemistry, and medicine, people's capability to drastically alter the natural environment had vastly increased. However, inducing natural change often ends up requiring more time, the assignment of more people, and the expenditure of more money than was expected. Since these resources could be utilized differently, the question arises whether their employment to effect the natural change is best for the organism as a whole. Answering this question to the extent possible by analyzing the optimum allocation of available resources is the basic contribution of comprehensive planning discussed in the previous chapter.

As a general rule, the focus and condition of nature should be modified by human change as little as possible to achieve a designated purpose, and only with great care and forethought. If there is not enough information to confidently project the major consequences of human intervention, formulation of specific plans should be deferred. The plans of the Brazilian government in 1970 "to integrate the Amazon region into the rest of the country" are a case in point:

> The Transamazon Highway was designed to accomplish three main goals. . . . a safety valve for the poverty-striken Northeast. . . . fill a demographic void in a region occupying half of Brazil's territory. . . . create access to mineral and timber reserves. . . . The Transamazon scheme has largely failed on all three counts. . . . Planners need to pay closer attention to ecological factors such as the suitability of soils and proposed cultivars. (Smith, 1981)

Other forces and conditions of nature which were ignored or underestimated relate to the river system, topography, indigenous vegetation, resettlement areas, and public health aspects of migration.

> The Transamazon project fits a pattern of repeated failure of government-directed settlement schemes in South America. . . . Blueprints are usually drawn up with little or no understanding of the ecological and cultural conditions of settlement areas. Bureaucratic controls [human changes] often hamper the development of colonization zones. (Smith, 1981)

Other things being equal, comprehensive planning achieves the best results for the organism with which it is concerned when it does not oppose or transgress natural change, but conforms to, works with, or utilizes natural forces and constraints to the fullest extent possible. The choice between chemical pesticides and biological predators in agricultural pest control represents this alternative. Subdivision and land development of urban hillside areas can conform to the existing terrain, or it can require massive earth movement, change in the drainage pattern, and other alterations of the environment. Organizational plans in the business world to increase human productivity can be based on the innate self-interest of employees, or on ignoring this innate motivation, seeking to eliminate it, or successfully superimposing other values. The extent to which operations must await natural change in weather conditions is an ever-present consideration in contingency plans of the military services, and in the operating plans of air carriers. Even in catastrophes of storm, fire, flood, famine, and pestilence when maximum human action is imperative regardless of longer-range consequences, emergency plans are most effective when they are formulated in accord with the natural forces involved.

Since natural change is inherent in the physical world, it can be modified but rarely eliminated or fundamentally altered. Human change, on the other hand, is the product of human choice: however necessary or desirable it is deemed to be. Each of these changes comprises a sequence or "curve" of diminishing incremental effects ranging from the most impactful to the least consequential. The most extreme planning policy would call for no interventional effects by the other. Nature would evolve untouched by human change; human activities would continue unrestricted regardless of their cumulative effect on the natural environment. Most people agree that this extreme planning policy is neither desirable nor possible because both natural and human change are almost always involved even in programs intended to achieve only one of them. Striking the best balance is analytically difficult because natural and human change are mutually supportive or conflictive depending on circumstances. The common point must be identified on the two "curves" of diminishing incremental impact that represents the optimum balance of their combined cause and effect.

Residential land development of hillside areas in the United States illustrates the two extreme and the intermediate positions. A planning policy of retaining the natural environment for its intrinsic and recreational values leaves the hillside terrain largely undisturbed as open space, recreational area, or park. The natural processes of drainage, erosion, storm damage, and vegetation are left alone except as necessary to control any adverse effects on surrounding built-up land, prevent hazardous conditions, and allow recreational use.

A planning policy allowing the housing market to determine development, thereby maximizing tax revenue, results in extensive earth movement to re-shape the terrain into the maximum number of building sites for which there is demonstrable demand, with primary and secondary street systems providing easy access. The natural vegetation stripped during the earth movement and grading is replaced by whatever ground cover, shrubs, and trees individual property owners see fit or are required to plant.

The intermediate planning policy is a combination of providing needed housing and retaining environmental features. Earth movement and density of development are restricted to retain certain areas in their natural state: as unused open space; "greenbelts," "vest-pocket," local, or regional parks; or other open land uses. Population density and traffic flow are balanced by design. Building restrictions are imposed to prevent highrise or other types of construction which would impair the visual quality of the land development as a whole and the appearance of areas emphasizing the natural terrain.

This intermediate policy introduces the human change considered desirable from the viewpoint of comprehensive planning, or believed to be politically necessary, while at the same time retaining as many natural features as feasible. It represents the point of best balance between the progressively diminishing returns of overemphasizing either natural or human change.

Objective. . . .
1. Of or pertaining to an object of action or feeling; forming an object of attraction, or a final cause. . . .

Object. . . .
4. That by which the mind, or any of its activities, is directed; that on which the purposes are fixed as the end of action and effort; that which is sought for; end; aim; final cause. . . .

(*Webster's New International Dictionary of the English Language,* Second Edition (Unabridged), 1960, Vol. II, p. 1679)

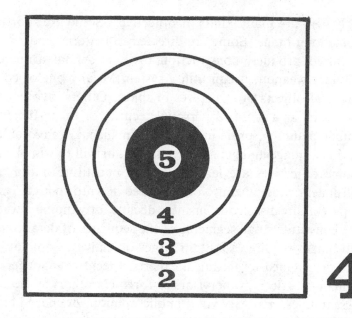

OBJECTIVES
Dependent Variables

LIFE IS FULL OF objectives, set by people in connection with their personal affairs and required by daily activities. And so it is in planning; the word itself indicates action or accomplishment toward some end. Defined broadly, objectives are to be found or are reflected in every part of all plans and all programs of effectuation. Goals, policies, planning objectives, and planning programs—as defined in the first chapter of this book—are particular kinds of objectives important in comprehensive planning. Of these, planning objectives are the most significant because in each case they represent conclusive analysis, decision, commitment of resources, and specific programs of intended accomplishment.

There are many kinds of objectives. Some are short-range, some long-range. Some are directed to material ends: a manufactured product, construction project, spatial arrangement, military weapon, urban utility system, or any one of countless physical objects or structures in space. Others involve intangibles such as a sense of personal security or of participation in public planning, pride in good workmanship, a favorable institutional image and general reputation, or will to win in combat. Some objectives are large-scale and constitute major accomplishments: revitalizing a deteriorated downtown area, reversing a potentially disastrous business decline, or winning a war. Others constitute small segments of the sequence of detailed accomplishment required to attain larger objectives. Some objectives are determined by technical experts, executive managers, commanding officers, supervisors or foremen; others by elected representatives, majority vote, public opinion, or special interests. Because the multitude and variety of objectives are without limit, both their discussion and employment in comprehensive planning require careful definition.

If asked to outline the planning process, most planners today place setting objectives as the first step, with the rest of the process derived from this initial statement. And they are correct to the extent that implicit or explicit objectives are always part of planning since the word itself is purposive by definition.

In the United States, the Soviet Union, and most countries around the world, setting objectives in local government planning means formulating master plans depicting a desired end-state for the municipality or region twenty to twenty-five years in the future. (Branch, 1981; Pallot, Shaw; Karachi Development Authority) This projection usually represents the hope or desire of the professional planning staff rather than the preference of the body politic and a governmental commitment for the future.

These end-state plans take the form of maps showing the land use and ground transportation system for the future city or region with a designated or assumed population. They are not correlated with the resources of people, time, and money that are available when the plans are formulated and will be available in the future to carry it out. They do not take into account essential socioeconomic, political, and financial realities, nor technological and engineering potentialities and limitations. Such plans are more false hopes than deliberate intentions.

In the past it was possible to attain fixed objectives by end-state master plans. As Czar of the Russians, Peter the Great could plan, build, and populate his new capital St. Petersburg (Leningrad) in the marshes of the Neva River delta within a few years, by enormous expenditure of money from taxes imposed on the populace and conscription of both labor and materials. Napoleon III could order his Prefect, Baron Georges Eugène Haussmann, to literally cut a crisscross pattern of straight avenues through the built-up structure of Paris, without regard for remnant parcels and their dispossessed or disturbed owners. Large projects for royal and religious rulers requiring vast resources and extensive planning were commonplace. The attitudes and desires of the populace could be ignored, heavy taxes and forced labor could be imposed. Even private enterprises, such as the Fuggers in late medieval Germany or the East India Company from the 16th to the 19th century, often operated under governmental auspices or privileges which enabled them to establish fixed objectives and undertake end-state plans impossible in more competitive situations.

The context for planning is very different today. Populations have increased in size many times. Despite the numerous places of severe poverty and even starvation in the world, average family income and individual freedom are appreciably greater than they were for the most part in the past. The economic and social needs and desires of people cannot be ignored. Political considerations must be taken into account even by authoritarian regimes. Societies in general are far more technically and organizationally complex than those of yesteryear. These are some of the reasons why fixed, long-range, end-state objectives are no longer feasible in comprehensive planning to the extent they have been in the past.

The widespread contention by planners that established objectives are the first requirement in the comprehensive planning process is in part the result of wide differences in what is meant by the word objectives. Some mean what are defined as goals at the beginning of this book: "general desires or intentions whose achievement is so hopeful, distant, and indefinite that they cannot be formulated and programmed with sufficient specificity to be incorporated quantitatively in the comprehensive plan." Goals so defined can indeed be set as the first step in planning since they are only broadly suggestive and readily subject to change. No specific commitments have been made. The same is true of policies which are "desirable developments" or "general approaches or directions."

Planning objectives as defined in this book are "statements of intention that have been identified, analyzed, and expressed with sufficient specificity to indicate how they can be accomplished within the time and resources available to the organism." They are the objectives of greatest importance in describing and conducting comprehensive planning. Because they are specific intentions and commitments, they cannot be set until the resources available and means of implementation are analyzed. When resources or considerations change by choice or circumstance, planning objectives must be altered accordingly. They are not goals or policies which can remain unaltered through considerable changes in conditions.

The business world has always been too volatile to contemplate corporate planning that sets fixed end-state objectives that cannot be revised immediately or changed completely on short notice, for according to Murphy's Law: If anything can go wrong, it will. Military planning, on the other hand, defines a set of specific strategies, tactical situations, and contingencies that are projected or assumed with respect to prospective adversaries.

The process of ascertaining the feasibility and programming the attainment of planning objectives is interactive or "circular": in that all determinant considerations in the analytical loop of interconnection between feasible objectives and available resources must be consistent with each other. In this sense, *comprehensive planning objectives are "dependent variables": dependent on the other elements and considerations in the analytical loop, and therefore subject to frequent change. They cannot be selected as a matter of presumptive preference without reference to the reality of their effectuation.*

Planning objectives are closely related to time, not only by the program of effectuation which each incorporates, but also among themselves as a group of different objectives defining the comprehensive planning activity of the organism in the future. There is the sequence for their accomplishment in time: a form of critical path scheduling in which one planning objective promotes the successful attainment of several or many others.

Fixed objectives can be set for individual projects or subsystems if the end product can be specifically stated, if the intent to achieve it is firm, and if the resources to realize it have been allocated and programmed. The projects undertaken by technically complex societies take longer and longer to design and build: utility systems, power plants, new aircraft, advanced military weapons systems, or reorganization of administrative units becoming larger on the average. Determining what to do, allocating or obtaining the necessary resources, preliminary design, plans, working drawings and specifications, approvals, financial arrangements, construction, and final certification often take more than ten years. To the extent comprehensive planning for the organism as a whole involves such projects, the fixed objectives they require constitute a larger and larger part of the overall planning process.

It should be noted, however, that the most fixed formulations of end-state objectives are subject invariably to some change. For example, during the process of building construction or other forms of closely scheduled effectuation, there are always small adjustments, substitutions, or changes that are made because it is impossible to conceive of every single component and operation in perfect sequence, and external events can and do occur which could not possibly be foreseen. So inevitable are such relatively minor changes that they are classified as change orders in construction projects, modifications in manufacturing processes, and mark numbers in military weapons production.

As technology and human activities become more complex, it becomes increasingly difficult to plan large projects which are designated as fixed planning objectives by comprehensive planning. Witness the widespread problems encountered in the United States in recent years in building nuclear power plants which have cost billions of dollars in overruns, years of delay, and even abandonment of facilities with enormous sunk costs. Serious operational problems have plagued many military weapons systems planned as special projects constituting planned objectives. Many corporate diversification plans when realized have turned out to be so unmanageable, incompatible, or unprofitable that they have been rescinded in whole or in part. The changes instigated during the prosecution of unsuccessful projects are if anything more numerous and impactful than if they were successful. And project failures require revisions in comprehensive planning to minimize their adverse effects and take into account the resources wasted.

Integration. . . . Act or process of integrating. . . .
1. To form into a whole; to make entire; to
complete; to round out; to perfect.
2. To unite (parts or elements), so as to form a
whole; also, to unite (a part or element) with
something else, esp. something more inclusive.
3. To indicate the whole of; to give the sum total
of. . . .

Element. . . .
3. One of the constituent parts, principles,
materials, or traits of anything, that is: one of the
relatively simple forms or units which enter variously
into a complex substance or thing (as bricks are
elements of a wall; cells are elements of living
bodies); or one of the simplest parts or principles of
which anything consists or into which it may be
analyzed. . . .

(*Webster's New International Dictionary of the English
Language,* Second Edition (Unabridged), 1960, Vol. II,
p. 1290; Vol. I, p. 829)

PRIMARY ELEMENTS

Integration

LIKE ALL PHENOMENA, the functioning of human organisms depends on the integration of constituent parts. Nothing exists that is totally indivisible and totally independent; every force and act interrelates with some other force or act. Integration of the constituent parts of organisms is therefore not only essential for their existence, but also fundamental to their planning. And since nothing exists that is absolutely instantaneous, this coordination of elements always involves an interval of time: a continuum of past, present, and future.

Without integration, the actions of different parts of human organisms are fragmented or even conflictive. With coordination, available resources can be applied most effectively toward prescribed goals and objectives. Many more parts of organisms can be identified than can be successfully integrated, because all but the simplest are composed of a multitude of components ranging from the broadest considerations to the infinitely minute, from the amorphous to the tangible, from the highly uncertain to the highly probable, from the quantifiable to the unquantifiable. A selection must be made of those relatively few elements or categories of closely related elements (subsystems) that are most determinant of the functioning of the organism. It is impossible with present knowledge to integrate all identifiable elements and aspects. There are always elements insufficiently understood for systematic treatment.

It is also impractical and uneconomic to attempt even a degree of planning so complete that the time and cost required are excessive. That degree of planning is desirable that "pays for itself" by increasing the current efficiency or longer-range effectiveness of the organism, or by reducing the number of mistakes which would otherwise probably have been made.

> . . . Methods of foresight and coordination are costly in themselves, except they may be of the common sense variety. Calculations, blueprints, statistical research, and actuarial processes are expensive . . . so that they cannot be applied economically to many problems which are important in the aggregate . . . the question usually has two aspects, the cost of money and the cost of delay. The latter is frequently much the more important . . . every responsible person in any sort of organized effort, as well as in purely personal affairs, often experiences great difficulty in determining whether it is expedient to await or to secure further information. . . . (Barnard)

In business, the economic benefit of actions resulting specifically from the integration of information and analysis performed in comprehensive corporate planning can usually be
identified by observation and judgment if not by specific dollar
figures. But the usefulness of the planning process in preventing
costly errors is far more difficult to evaluate since the necessary
comparative event never occurred and the extent of the probable error and its effects can only be estimated. And there are important considerations to which it is difficult or impossible to
ascribe monetary value. For example, employee contentment is
only partially measured by labor turnover, union relations, and
grievance procedures; a trademark or business goodwill is usually given the arbitrary value of one dollar; the value of the recrea-
tion provided in parks or the culture in museums cannot be
measured in dollars and cents for city planning. Thus, a consensus of the most informed judgment available is the only measure
for certain aspects and benefits of comprehensive planning,
since it must deal as best it can with all the significant elements
of the organism, including the intangible. Only measurable and
comparable quantities can be evaluated statistically.

The significant elements to be integrated in manufacturing
enterprises include marketing and advertisement, production,
sales and distribution, finance, personnel, research and development. Production may in turn be broken down into material
and labor, manufacturing, quality control, and shipping. Most
local governments are organized into departments: finance, fire,
police, sanitation, building and safety, transportation, public
works, public health, social services—each representing a primary responsibility of the municipality or county. For tactical
operations, an army is constituted of squads, platoons, companies, battalions, regiments, divisions, corps, and armies; for
logistics: quartermaster, ordnance, engineering, signal corps,
and transportation. As an example of project organization,

building construction is often divided into: site preparation, foundations, framing, masonry, plumbing, electrical, roofing, glazing, heating and ventilation, plastering, finish carpentry, and painting.

The functioning of organisms in nature also involves primary elements. The form of physical matter is determined by the relative position and interaction of its fundamental particles. Various categories of animals and plants have dominant characteristics most descriptive of their nature and most vital to their existence. And although every microscopic component of physical man and woman interacts with every other, certain organs or anatomical systems are primary. Cardinal elements are seldom of precisely equal significance; although all are essential, some are functionally dominant. At times a normally minor element may have such a temporary impact that it becomes the determinant force for change.

Operating conjointly, the primary elements define the organism with the simplification necessary for managerial purposes, determine for the most part its development, and serve as the best means for its manipulation and comprehensive planning. The primary elements of human organisms are usually identified by experience and judgment. For animate and inanimate organisms in the physical and biological worlds, this ordering of parts is revealed by scientific observation, knowledge, or experiment.

The primary elements will vary according to the type and level of planning and the managerial viewpoint. In manufacturing, the production engineer concentrates on such spatial matters as the general circulation of materials and people, the type and arrangement of machines, the space required for separate operations. The human factors engineer focuses on additional elements affecting physical performance, morale, and productivity: noise levels, eye strain, unnatural bodily movements, rest rooms, rest periods, or attitude towards management. To increase productivity, the most efficient mechanistic arrangements may require modification to fit the physiological and psychological needs of employees. The relative importance of these two aspects will vary according to the degree of automation, but of course both are always present. Overall human guidance, programming, supervision, and maintenance are required even in the most trouble-free robotian processes.

The elements of outstanding significance for comprehensive planning also depend on the method of operation of the organism, its goals, and technology. Comparison of automation today with its form in the early 1900s illustrates the effects of all three of these factors. At the turn of the present century, the primary consideration for production planning layout was the individual worker, his machine, and work station; today it is the mechanized assembly line itself: with its conveyors, specialized subassembly, automatic machines, and mechanized quality control. The parallel change of objective from higher quality, more durable products to cheaper, limited life, or disposable products has made high volume, standardization, and speed essential elements of mass production. And new technological developments—sophisticated television monitors, robots, remote sensors, computer control—have taken their place in production planning.

The particular situation or stage of development of the organism also influences the primary elements for integrated planning. If a private enterprise has poor cash flow, minimal operating reserves, and no capital reserves, then the immediate primary objective is correcting this precarious financial situation by accumulating the monetary resources needed for operating changes or new facilities. Usually, some improvements can be made which do not require additional capital or jeopardize the narrow profit margin for survival. But changes which will increase efficiency and earnings in the longer-run ordinarily require some cushion of capital or surplus reserves to finance substantial improvements or support a period of reduced profits during a production changeover.

Military planners are constantly confronted with a comparable problem: maintaining or strengthening existing military forces until they are superseded at some future time by improved military power. For example:

> The easy way [for General Curtiss LeMay, Commanding General of the U.S. Strategic Air Command in 1954] to make the transition between planes would have been to simply fly the B-50s away from one airfield, fly the B-36s in and give all the crews at that field the six months of intensive training needed to learn to fly the B-36 in combat. This, however, would have cut one whole group off the combat-ready list. So LeMay has performed an incredible job of juggling, keeping the B-50s, the B-36s and all the training programs in the air at once. He will soon get the first models of the successor to the B-36, a new, much faster and far superior all-jet heavy bomber, the B-52. These too will be folded into the program without losing a single day of readiness for a single plane. (Haverman)

The same situation exists today in connection with the introduction of new generations of guided missiles, aircraft, methods of aiming and guidance, nuclear artillery, tanks, submarines and other naval vessels, and every other weapon system and military operation.

Countries at an early stage of economic development confront a basic choice between the primary elements required to achieve the planning objective of rapid industrialization and those required for gradual modernization. The decision of most of these countries to industrialize to the fullest extent possible as quickly as possible emerged from the flow of revenues to the Oil

Producing and Exporting Countries (OPEC) beginning in 1973, and to other nations with natural resources needed by more highly developed countries. Many nations that elect rapid industrialization experience problems they did not anticipate or chose to ignore: cultural shock, religious antagonism, income disparities, disruptive migration from rural areas to cities, poverty and insecurity, or political instability. Fewer problems are experienced by countries planning to achieve the same objective of economic development more gradually by labor intensive projects designed to lead in time to mechanized production. Related economic, social, cultural, religious, political, and attitudinal problems are less severe because there is more time for their gradual resolution. However, capital formation and the development of some national objectives will be delayed.

If the primary elements required to adequately represent the functioning of the organism are too numerous or too complex to integrate successfully, they are reduced to the number that can be coordinated analytically, formed into related groups, or considered sequentially. Of course, separating and subdividing intellectual-analytical processes into comprehensible arrangements has been employed by humankind throughout history. It is the way sensory stimulation and response occur biologically and electrochemically in the brain and nervous system of animals. It is part of scientific method. In management science, one method of articulating related parts is formulating a "logical tree" or "branching."

Normally, each subdivisional unit of intellectual-analytical consideration is also a distinct unit of operational activity, administrative organization, and planning. Division into manageable parts is the basic principle of organizing human activities. Formal arrangements are shown on organization charts and chains of command, but informal relationships that do not appear on organization charts (the grapevine) may be crucial to the successful conduct of the activity. When no prior experience exists, pyramids of administrative organization are developed from the bottom up. Functional groupings and levels of administration are formulated which will optimize achievement of the designated end product.

Correlation varies with the several chronological stages of planning. There is integration in preliminary planning to determine whether to proceed with a particular objective or project. At this initial stage, approximate data and conditional assumptions may be enough to reach conclusions based on experience and subjective judgment. A decision to proceed ushers in a second stage of more thorough formulation and confirmation, with more specific selection and integration of primary elements. The most complete coverage and the greatest precision are reserved for the third stage when planning objectives are formulated with their programs of accomplishment. The appropriate primary elements are identified at each stage of development and organizational level.

Planning a construction project is illustrative. The stage of preliminary evaluation and decision to proceed considers such primary elements as: financial capability; type, size, and general characteristics of the physical entity required to produce the desired end product; location and land acquisition; approximate cost and time of construction; continuing costs of maintenance during the probable life of the structure. The second stage involves thorough preliminary design of the proposed structure and more precise calculation of the elements included in the first stage as they relate to this more detailed design. The final plans developed in the third stage add working drawings and specifications, a construction schedule, precise cash flow requirements for the various project costs, and administrative plans for the managerial direction of the project and construction supervision. Architects and engineers use the terms "schematics," "preliminaries," and "working drawings and specifications" for these three stages in designing a structure, but this does not in-

Comprehensive Planning Process		Specific Illustration (Building a House)
Objectives	Requirements	Protection from the elements (rain and moisture, cold, heat, etc.); minimum space and its division; sanitary facilities; light and air . . .
	Desires	Size and number of rooms and other spaces; materials; appearance; various features . . .
Resources		Money and credit, labor materials, and time available . . .
Situation	Internal	Anticipated family income and method of financing; present and anticipated size and composition of family; way of life and its relation to design . . .
	External	Site features; local climate; orientation and immediate surroundings; public transportation and schools available nearby . . .
Primary Elements		Money; lot; rooms and various spaces and enclosures; materials; aesthetics . . .
Principal Interrelationships		Relation of different rooms and spaces to each other; cost of space versus cost of materials, construction methods, and special features . . .
Representation of the Entirety		Topographic lot survey; preliminary drawings and plans; scale model; specifications; cost estimates, verbal descriptions by architect . . .
Reappraisal of Primary Elements and Consideration of Second-Order Elements and Interrelationships		Change in number of rooms, materials, or other primary features because of cost; selection of those special features possible within the budget . . .
		Specific heating, electrical, water, and plumbing systems; details of framing and foundation construction, and their effect on plan arrangement . . .
Projection		Plans showing possible future modification or expansion of house, or further development of lot space; provisions for inaccessible repair and maintenance . . .
Decision-making and Project Plan		Blueprints; final specifications; building permit; construction contracts . . .
Adjustment; Feedback		Changes made during construction; revision of construction blueprints; occupancy certificate.

Building a House as a Familiar Example of Essential Steps in the Comprehensive Planning Process

clude additional considerations such as affordability and cost of construction and maintenance, which are essential elements of project planning by the client organization.

When the effectuation of a plan is under way, the final phase of integration begins. Elements and aspects come to light that were missed or unpredicted in the first three stages of project planning. If the project is complex, with a multitude of design considerations and complicated construction, it cannot be conceived in advance in complete and final detail. Furthermore, the time required to effectuate the project plan may produce changes in the cost and time of delivering materials, in the availability of labor, or delay and disruption because of adverse weather or other unpredictable environmental impacts. Only the simplest plans, largely immune to external effects, can be drawn so completely and reliably that some modification is not necessary or desirable during their implementation. These modifications comprise an additional primary element added to project planning during the fourth stage of effectuation.

Because the elements and interactions that constitute organisms are inextricably linked, *the primary elements cannot be understood until their interrelationships are generally comprehended.* It is the limits of human comprehension—not the nature of organisms—that required separate consideration of elements and interactions. Identifying and understanding a tiny fraction of the infinite number of primary elements and interactions in the universe constitutes most of human knowledge. Three categories of interrelationship between elements are involved in the integration required in comprehensive planning: direct, indirect, and remote.

In direct relationships cause and effect are functionally and temporally immediate. They do not act through intermediate causal connections or analytical considerations: electromagnetic storms on the sun and wireless communication noise on earth; precipitation and ground conditions; land use and transportation; accounting changes and financial transactions; the destructive effects of military weapons; or adjustments in human behavior to conform to legislation. Illustrations abound.

Indirect relationships take place through several readily identifiable intermediate steps: raw materials into finished product; sanitary utility systems and public health; a vaccine and immunity; neighborhood condition and mortgage lending; sale of surplus material in one country and the price of the same material newly mined in another country; military blockade and surrender.

Remote interrelationships occur through an extended sequence of repercussive connections: visual characteristics of neighborhoods and social behavior; management organization and return on investment; military spending and agricultural prices; global effects of localized environmental pollution. Remote interrelationships are not a function of spatial separation, although geographical distance has acted to increase remoteness throughout history.

These three categories of interaction are also exemplified by the sequential consequences of a single force or event. At the atomic level, expansion and contraction of matter relate directly to other materials with which it is connected, indirectly to the functioning of the product of which it is part, and remotely to the reputation and business success of the producer. A new traffic regulation affects drivers directly and immediately, citywide traffic flow indirectly, and air pollution remotely. A change in interest rates influences business borrowing directly and immediately, financial condition indirectly, and employee productivity remotely. The instantaneous destructiveness of a military weapon is direct to say the least. Indirectly, it affects the immediate environment in many other ways. And it relates remotely to the outcome of the conflict of which it is a tiny part.

The relative significance of elements is not a function of the level of organization. An element in comprehensive planning at the top is not necessarily more important to the organism than an element at a lower level. For example, in a community with most lots the same size, and with an established apartment design covering the entire buildable area of the lot which developers consider the only economically feasible arrangement, increasing the width of parking stalls in the garage as little as six inches to make it easier to get in and out of cars can have a pronounced deterrent effect on rental housing construction—so much so that the increased width of parking stalls becomes an important element of city planning. In military planning, an unexpected enemy breakthrough in a small but key sector of the battlefield can threaten its total collapse, necessitating immediate revision of tactical plans and any corresponding adjustment required in strategic plans; such an occasion occurred at the Battle of the Bulge toward the end of World War II. A technological advancement in a small low-level unit of a company that significantly alters the prospects of its product line may call for revision of the primary elements of corporate planning. Needless to say, the likelihood of unforeseen developments adds to the difficulties of comprehensive planning.

The type or category of interrelationship does not correlate with geographical distance. The world is tied together as never before: by modern means of communication, international trade and monetary transactions, multinational corporations and cartels, foreign business subsidiaries and manufacturing plants, global military systems. Foreign relations are certainly a primary element in comprehensive planning by national governments. For some of the larger corporations in the United States which derive the largest percentage of their profits from foreign operations, monetary exchange rates require continual attention, so much so that they may constitute a primary element of corporate planning. All organizations engaged in international business must be prepared for a wide range of unforeseen developments that may vitally affect profitability or even survival:

political changes increasing taxes, establishing quotas, or initiating expropriation; changes in the cost of essential raw materials produced abroad; bureaucratic inefficiency. Global elements are critical in planning military weapons systems such as long-range aircraft, missiles, nuclear submarines, or the United States Army Readiness Command. Non-human organisms may have primary elements far removed spatially or geographically: for example, migratory animals and plants pollinated by insects. Even inorganic material may have spatially separated primary elements.

Human judgment is the most powerful and practical means of integration in comprehensive planning. It incorporates accumulated experience, observation, and study. It can comprehend a great variety of information. Its conscious and preconscious memory bank is impressive. It embodies analytical capabilities of the mind that are both inherited and acquired. It can consider with integrative intent elements that cannot be measured or do not share any common unit of measurement, intangibles as well as tangibles, indefinites as well as definites, probabilities, both important and less important elements and aspects. The intelligent mind can conceptualize the past, present, and future in a single scan, recognize, visualize and imagine may different pictorial images and geographical representations. It can comprehend and consider the critical procedural steps in comprehensive planning and other relevant elements and aspects discussed in this book.

Of course, objective rational thought may be flawed by obstructive self-interest, ingrained prejudices and biases, emotional overreaction, disruptive unconscious drives, illusions and delusions, and at times hysteria. A small group of knowledgeable people working together constructively constitutes the best means of integrating different elements in comprehensive planning, provided they do not allow some strongly held view to dominate or only the lowest common denominator to emerge.

This collective brainpower is strengthened by using people who can contribute diverse knowledge, experience, and analytical capabilities, take the longer-range as well as the shorter-range view, subordinate self-interest to the best interest of the organism being planned, and recognize their own unconstructive overreactions. Although computers can perform certain analytical operations with numbers far faster than man, none can approach his observational and judgmental capabilities, especially those that apply to the coordination of diverse activities and considerations.

Judgment is certainly less subjective and more objective and reliable when there are common units of measurement for different elements that permit their numerical-mathematical comparison. Since the monetary unit is the most universal unit of correlation available today, it is widely used for this purpose. Efforts are being made to reduce its well-known limitations by extending the range of monetary measurement. But there are always elements and aspects of comprehensive planning that cannot be meaningfully measured in dollars or other currency: aesthetics, attitudes, morale, intentions, personal capabilities and prejudices, and other quantitatively elusive but important components. For certain subsystems or combinations of several components, particular units of measurement are employed: morbidity and mortality rates for health service, health insurance, and risk analysis, British Thermal Units (BTUs) for comparative energy planning, or the kill probability to determine the relative lethality of military weapons systems.

Pure numbers without associative reference are used when they are sufficient for the planning purpose: total inquiries received concerning various products, military personnel in the armed services of different nations, or intersections in different urban street systems. Further refinement of such numerical totals requires an additional level of classification. And relating each of these additional categories more conclusively to comprehensive planning for the organism as a whole requires some unit of measurement and comparison more specifically indicative than aggregate numbers.

The human mind is remarkably adept at recognizing, appraising, and comparing pictorial and graphical representations of many kinds. General and particular similarities and differences in size, scale, dimension, form, pattern, arrangement, density, and other spatial attributes are noted immediately. This perception permits evaluation and comparison of elements and aspects of planning that can only be portrayed or best expressed and comprehended as pictures, drawings, diagrams, or other graphical representations. For example: the pattern of different kinds of streets, railroads, pipelines, waterways, and other transportation routes comprising an urban circulation system; complete organization charts for large corporations; the global, theater, or battlefront disposition of combat and military support units. Although computer graphics are well developed, it is unlikely that pattern recognition by computer or more advanced electromagnetic scanning will ever come close to the scope, depth, inclusiveness, and subtlety of human visual perception and comprehension.

Successful integration of primary elements in comprehensive planning requires another analytical step best performed by human judgment. Rarely are these elements of equal importance, and rarely can their relative significance be determined by some method of calculation more rigorous, scientific, or accurate than human judgment. So many disparate or unquantifiable considerations are involved that human judgment alone can decide the necessary comparative "weighting." This is often illustrated by environmental impact statements which may include such disparate elements as the location of endangered biological species and animal life, archaeological and cultural sites, existing and proposed land usage, transportation systems, and aesthetics. There is no way that these effects can now be calculated and compared with quantitative precision.

When primary elements can be expressed in numbers, mathematical-statistical integration provides the additional dimension of quantitative comparison, determination of probabilities, extrapolation, regression analysis, and other calculations. In the business world, most operations and objectives can be quantified and expressed in monetary units. Profit, adequate return on investment, and organizational survival are simpler and easier to state in numbers than the objectives of military and governmental planning. Mathematical models representing the business enterprise as a whole or several of its parts can be formulated for comprehensive planning purposes. And although they are never totally complete, they can usefully simulate the business for corporate planning purposes.

This is difficult or impossible to do in military planning even though its objective of victory or of surviving any conflict can be clearly stated. But some of its vital components cannot be quantified: military morale, hostile intentions, the reliability and value of military intelligence concerning potential adversaries, the performance of complex weapon systems in actual combat, weather conditions. Civil governmental planning involves multiple goals and objectives responsive to many societal groups and special interests. These goals and objectives may change rapidly and frequently. Legislative decisions, political actions, economic conditions near and far, and environmental effects can neither be defined nor foreseen, much less numerically calculated. Such indefinite but impactful elements or situations involved in civil governmental planning cannot be modelled with mathematical precision.

The overall informational and analytical statement that constitutes a comprehensive plan—the Representation of the Entirety, Principle 8—includes material on the internal and external environmental situation; available and potential resources of humanpower, money, and time; present and projected states of the major components of the organism, separately and in combination; and relevant considerations that cannot be quantified but must be taken into account. To perform this analysis and make this complex set of interrelated data comprehensible, the information must be organized according to the primary elements selected.

Projection. . . .
1. Act of throwing or shooting forward; state of
being projected; also, ejection.
2. A scheming or planning; rarely, that which is
planned; contrivance; design; as the *projection* of a
new railroad. . . .

Project. . . .
1. To throw or cast forward. . . .
2. To cast about or revolve in the mind; to contrive;
devise, scheme; as, to *project* a plan. . . .

(*Webster's New International Dictionary of the English
Language,* Second Edition (Unabridged), 1960, Vol. II,
p. 1078)

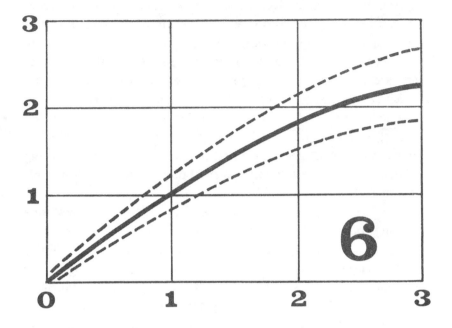

PROJECTION

Separate and Unified

PROJECTION IS THE ACT of "throwing or casting forward." *A planning projection is an analytical extension
of the past and present into the future for the purposes of
comprehensive planning.* In order to plan it is necessary to visualize, or anticipate what is likely to occur in the future as a consequence of natural changes and purposeful human actions. Together with change and integration, *projection is a fundamental
characteristic of the comprehensive planning process.*

Since time is continuous, there is no absolute chronological
present time; there is only past and future. There is a comparative present representing the chronological relationship between

a given instant and a given condition or event, and a concurrent present equating forces and events simultaneously in time and space. There is the operational present of human affairs, which may vary from a few days to several years depending on what activities, events, or forces are involved. It is the time during which conditions remain relatively unchanged: a period of evolutionary stability or ecological equilibrium; an interval when no further human changes are contemplated; or simply a limited time covering the recent past and the immediate future, serving an operational purpose, such as the budget year. Projection refers to future time beyond the present.

Projections are based on past experience. They may be one of a number of forms of extrapolation from what has occurred in the past. They may be an extension by analogy with a similar phenomenon which has an observed history of predictable consequences from causal mechanisms created through the long process of geological and biological evolution. In this sense, every voluntary and involuntary act of humankind involves explicit and implicit projections. Were this not so, there could be no involuntary evolutionary advance nor purposive human activity. Without past history to provide a basis for extrapolation, projections are judgments derived from whatever logic can be applied successfully or from intuitive best guess. Once a record of reliable projection is established, it can of course be continued with greater confidence.

Although no future event can be predicted with absolute certainty, there are of course a multitude of predictions concerning physical phenomena which can be made with almost total reliability: the effects of gravity and the movement of celestial bodies, the action of thermodynamic and electrodynamic forces, or the reaction of chemical substances to changes of internal and external condition. However, some natural events global in nature and involving diverse physical forces—such as the weather and seismic activity—cannot be forecast with comparable reliability. Numerous biological organisms, including social insect societies, also act in closely predictable ways. Science sets for itself the criterion of "ability to predict." Physics, chemistry, biology, geology, and other sciences derive their intellectual validity and operational usefulness from the multitude of specific predictions that are made from theoretical formulations based on scientific observation and experiment.

> The Agriculture Department currently is using satellite measurement of crop acreage in its regular forecasts of foreign crop harvests. . . . A final analysis of the [experimental] results more than met the goal of being able to make crop estimates that would be 90% accurate 90% of the time. (Bishop)

When the predictive capabilities of science are applied to human activities, their accuracy is reduced. Political, legal, operationally practical, and cost considerations which are not part of the basic scientific investigation must be taken into account when derivative policies and regulations are established in the general public interest. For example, geological soil site surveys required before plans are drawn and building permits are issued, or the standards of structural strength developed from physics which must be met before working drawings are approved, can never be as rigorous as if there were no limits on cost or on politically acceptable governmental control. The degree of socially acceptable risk, discussed elsewhere in this book, is always involved.

Medicine applies the best prescriptive capabilities developed from anatomical, physiological, and psychological observation and experiment over many years. Engineering and other applied sciences do likewise. The levels of risk accepted for the regulation of human activities and products are greater than those that scientific experiment or analysis indicate could be attained by setting higher standards. Consequently, there will always be occasional structural engineering failures, medication with belatedly discovered adverse side effects, landslides from unforeseen geological failure, or floods above the maximum to be expected every 50 to 100 years based on the historical record. Unfortunately, the public and the news media remember the exceptional failure more than the high percentage of success.

Since weather commands such universal attention and is important for so many activities, the inaccuracies in forecasting which the public observes contribute to the widespread skepticism concerning prediction. But methods are available providing an 80–90 percent accuracy in predicting weather conditions a year or more in the future for many specific situations such as an important outdoor event, launching and landing an orbiting vehicle, or stream flow at a given point in a river basin. The same approximate range of accuracy is possible in forecasting temperature plus or minus 3F degrees on a weekly or annual basis, somewhat less in predicting precipitation. (Krick)

The lack of public confidence in projection is strengthened by the repeatedly unsuccessful attempts to project economic conditions, and the lack of consensus even as to how this should be done. Ironically, many of the socioeconomic developments that the ordinary citizen is most anxious to predict are the most unpredictable because of the numerous and diverse variables and intangibles involved that cannot now be projected separately, much less collectively.

There are several ways in which projection is applied. In selecting the best course of action initially, it is important to know the probable outcome of several alternatives. And the continued functioning of an existing activity depends on projections of the human, material, and financial resources it requires at different stages in the future. The activities of every individual—as well as those of civil governments, business, and the military—require at least minimum projection, explicit or implicit as the case may be.

Another kind of projection focuses on intent rather than expectation: the number of people to be hired by a business concern or enlisted in a military service during a forthcoming period; determination of how urban street maintenance will be carried out during the budget year; or any plan or program of action employing available resources. As this reference to available resources suggests, causal projections representing intent and those predicting what may happen cannot be completely separated. Invariably, the most thoroughly predetermined plans are based on certain expectations with respect to resources, operational situation, and environmental conditions; they are subject to revision or abandonment when the unexpected occurs. Causal and predictive projections are therefore differentiated not only by their different primary purpose, but also by the wide difference in the probability of their respective accuracy.

Projection is part of routine anticipatory activity: "the positive actions of procuring clothing, building shelters, etc., in advance of immediate need" (Barnard). Much of the work on a farm and those civil governmental, military, and business activities affected by the weather are organized in anticipation of seasonal conditions and needs. Provision for regular maintenance, overhaul, and replacement parts is an essential element of planning military weapons systems, civil governmental utility and transportation systems, and many commercial products.

Projection may be short- or long-term, depending on what is being planned and how far into the future reliable forethought can be extended. At one extreme, the public reception and rating of television programs are so volatile and unpredictable that producers and parent corporations must be ready and able to have programs cancelled overnight despite a large investment and expenditure of time and money making, testing, and selling the pilot. At the other extreme, plans for the tree farming previously referred to are projected sixty to seventy-five years into the future. Strategic military plans are by definition and use longer-range than tactical plans.

Whether planning projections are shorter- or longer-range may also be a matter of choice. In business, depreciation may be accelerated or drawn out. Oil producing nations may choose how they want to program their exhaustible resources: high production and immediate profits, or production and income spread out over a longer period of time. A city can plan its street maintenance expenditures over a shorter or longer period, depending on when it expects to receive revenues, subventions, or grants. A military operation may be planned as a blitzkrieg or a war of attrition lasting years. For all organisms, reaction to an emergency situation calls for immediate action and short-range operational plans. In each of these examples, the planning projections will be different dependent on the choice among alternative policies.

Contrary to common conception, effective planning is not contingent upon infallible, precise, or even highly accurate long-range projections. More vital to successful comprehensive planning is continual application of short-range projections to current decisions which must be made and cannot be postponed. In real life, the immediate future is more crucial than the distant future, for the continued functioning and survival of the organism depends on the essential needs of tomorrow more than probable or possible requirements of a more distant day. Long-range projections may be essential to guide the growth and development of the organism, but its continued existence is certainly a necessary precondition.

Many phenomena, unpredictable over any extended period of time, evolve so gradually that periodic short-range projections can be made. Wide variations in interest rates may be unpredictable over a period of many months or years, but they seldom change many percentage points in a week or several weeks. Urban land uses may change considerably over the years, but rarely during weeks. Military capabilities are not subject to rapid change apart from a natural catastrophe destroying military personnel or equipment. Even new weapons or other military breakthroughs take time to progress from research: to development, to production, distribution, training, and official adoption.

Most shorter-range projections are therefore more accurate than longer-range projections. The early stages of linear and nonlinear extrapolation are the most accurate. Consequently, the deductive conclusions which can be drawn for the near future are more reliable than those which can be derived for the more distant future. By definition, the effects of small forces which will bring about cumulative change are less in the near term than they will be when compounded later. Also, in general, inertia and the normal resistances to change discussed in the last chapter of this book mean that the immediate future will not be as different from the present and recent past as will be the case later on. Many socioeconomic phenomena, unpredictable over an extended period of time, develop so gradually that periodic short-range projections can be made with considerable accuracy. These provide the advance notice necessary for comprehensive planning purposes. Successive projections reveal unexpected changes in an established trend in time for short-range adjustments to be made. Successful planning for some activities requires frequent projections: weather, aircraft availability, and other information for planning airline operations; sales and inventory projections of peak load requirements for planning utility and various other services. Most planning calls for different ranges of projection for different elements and aspects of the organism.

The general direction of development disclosed by frequent short-range projection is sufficient for the effective planning of most socioeconomic organisms. But the continued functioning

PROJECTION, TIME, OUTCOME
Aspects of the Planning Process
(Opposite Page)

Diagrammatically illustrating normal planning development over time (i.e. without drastic changes of objective and direction, normal range of purposive change):

(1) Allowing for a range of expected variation in the reliability of projections,

(2) Reflecting changes of plan brought about by developments external to the operation plan,

(3) Providing for expected modifications of specific objective,

(4) Providing the general continuity of development necessary for the effective utilization of the resources applied to the endeavor,

(5) Insuring specific outcome (longer-range resultant development) consistent with the initial basic objectives and subsequent modifications.

Time Scale
[Intervale (0–1, 1–2, etc.)—Periodic Revision of Shorter-Range Operation Plans]

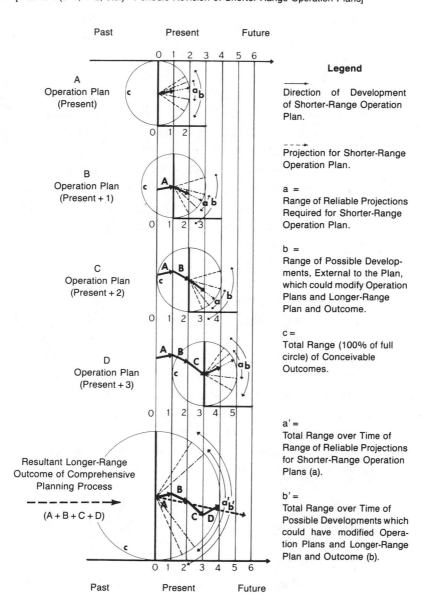

Past   Present   Future

A
Operation Plan
(Present)

B
Operation Plan
(Present + 1)

C
Operation Plan
(Present + 2)

D
Operation Plan
(Present + 3)

Resultant Longer-Range
Outcome of Comprehensive
Planning Process

(A + B + C + D)

Past   Present   Future

Legend

→
Direction of Development
of Shorter-Range Operation
Plan.

- - -→
Projection for Shorter-Range
Operation Plan.

a =
Range of Reliable Projections
Required for Shorter-Range
Operation Plan.

b =
Range of Possible Develop-
ments, External to the Plan,
which could modify Operation
Plans and Longer-Range
Plan and Outcome.

c =
Total Range (100% of full
circle) of Conceivable
Outcomes.

a' =
Total Range over Time of
Range of Reliable Projections
for Shorter-Range Operation
Plans (a).

b' =
Total Range over Time of
Possible Developments which
could have modified Opera-
tion Plans and Longer-Range
Plan and Outcome (b).

or survival of physical and physiological mechanisms may depend on projecting minute changes in pressure, chemical composition, permeability, temperature, or some other critical environmental condition. Fortunately, the different projections required for effectively planning each of these types of organism are those that can be made most reliably.

There are certain projections that can be made with greater confidence in the long-range: the next technological breakthrough after a recent advance in the state of the art, weather extremes, seismic disturbances, or the likelihood of nuclear war. Any one of these could happen, of course, in the near future, but the probability is greater for their occurrence at some unpredictable moment during a much longer period of time. In insurance, to project exactly the number of insurable deaths in the United States during the next week by age category and cause would be fortuitous. Statistical records show that the number of such deaths varies considerably during short intervals of time. Over a longer period these expected short-range fluctuations average out and a more predictable median trend can be established. But no insurance company would care to base its operations today on a projection of insurable deaths a hundred years hence. There are too many unpredictable developments or unforeseen events which could significantly alter the death rates during so long a time: advances in preventive and curative medicine, unexpected epidemics or changes in the food supply, unanticipated effects of environmental pollution. The safest projections for insurance lie between the extremely short-range and the very long-range.

There are various methods of projection embodied in budgets, plans, programs, surveys, estimates, and forecasts. Trends are extrapolated and conclusions drawn for the future from quantitative data concerning the past. Recorded and observed experience relating to a vast list of actions involving nature, social groups, and individual humans have been associated with expected results. History is available as general precedent for contemporary projections, provided past and present situations are comparable. Physical models of many kinds are constructed to simulate situations involving men, machines, and engineering systems so that their behavior can be studied experimentally and projected before plans are drawn and executed. There are also the more abstract models of mathematics, logic, financial accounting, and administrative organization, representing a given set of interrelationships and permitting a priori deductions concerning their effectiveness or probable behavior under different conditions and managerial decisions. Essential elements that represent human judgment rather than calculated consequences can be incorporated in these abstract models. And Delphi techniques provide the collective judgment of selected experts concerning what they believe will occur or can be brought about in the future.

All or various of these methods may be involved consciously or preconsciously in the individual human judgments with respect to the future that are so vital a part of the process of projection. '[Individual foresight] is largely an "intuitive" rather than a logical process. In the aggregate it is the most important of all known processes of foresight, and the least respected' (Barnard). Not only are such judgments inevitably involved in rational processes, but there are many situations and aspects in comprehensive planning for which no more definitive method exists. Most decisions with respect to human affairs must be made by intuitive judgment rather than scientific method. Employing the accumulated knowledge and the integrative and projective capabilities of the human mind, man reaches conclusions which he cannot derive by scientific method or some other formalized rational method. Most people do not realize how much integration and projection of consciously unremembered information stored in the preconscious mind occurs without their awareness. An intuitive judgment incorporates this hidden mental activity and possibly a genetically derived mind-set underlying constructive conclusions.

Infrequently noted but significant in this connection is the emotional make-up and condition of the individuals involved in formulating intuitive judgments which are the basis for formal action. Their judgments are impaired or invalidated to the extent they reflect unrecognized emotional overreactions irrelevant to the matter at hand. Occasionally, some neurotic drives may operate constructively in planning if they underlie and enhance certain useful perceptions. More often, they will prevent sound judgments whenever the subject under consideration triggers emotional overreaction. The more socially significant the organism, the greater the need for the soundest conclusion. These cautions apply to all elements of comprehensive planning, but they are especially pertinent to projection because it requires many individual and collective judgments extending present and proposed activities into the indefinite future.

The Joint Chiefs of Staff are an illustrative case in point. The four commanders of respectively the Air Force, Army, Navy, and Marines are jointly the principal military advisors to their commander-in-chief, the President of the United States, to the National Security Council, and the Secretary of Defense. Responsible for the highest technical-professional level of comprehensive military planning, their individual decisions and joint recommendations are of the greatest significance for the nation.

The same background information is available to each member for their group decisions. Their conclusions are the product of: (1) individual judgment, derived from experience, capacity to absorb and comprehend relevant information, analytical capability, and character structure, and (2) the interaction of individual judgments and personalities in the process of formulating a joint conclusion. Emotional overreaction can overshadow factual evidence in the formulation of personal judgments. Excessive loyalty to one of the four military services can subordinate the common cause.

> Air Force Gen. David Jones [Chairman of the Joint Chiefs of Staff] . . . proposed making his office the principal source of military advice to the President and Defense Secretary, and also suggested reducing the powers of the heads of the individual services. He said interservice rivalries long have hindered the making of an integrated military strategy. (*The Wall Street Journal,* February 1982)

The individual judgments of members of a group are affected or even formed by the opinion of other members during discussion. Irrational stubbornness, aggression, or "prima donna" persuasiveness may necessitate a compromise considered undesirable by the majority. The important point is that the psychological characteristics of group or committee members, performing individually and collectively, may decide the final resolution more than the most instructive analytical determination. Insofar as extraneous psychological dynamics produce results that would be different were they not present, the validity of the collective decision is impaired. From the viewpoint of comprehensive planning, the most capable individual talents do not necessarily function most successfully in a collective effort. In fact, less capable people who can function together constructively may develop a better consensus and reach sounder conclusions than more knowledgeable people who cannot work together successfully.

The projection of single phenomena and simpler organisms may be comparatively certain if the requisite data are available. But there is no established method of achieving this for phenomena and organisms composed of many disparate elements. Complex organisms can be projected with confidence if they act like others which are predictable, or function according to a single or several dominant and predictable elements. Illustrating the first of these, many results of medical research with animals can be successfully projected to humans. Illustrating the second, four gauges registering fuel supply, oil pressure, temperature, and battery charge predict the successful functioning of an automobile engine most of the time. And the opinions of a large population can be projected with a high degree of reliability from those of a very small scientifically selected sample of people.

The environmental context affecting every organism is difficult to anticipate for comprehensive planning purposes. At best, it is possible and practical to track only those external developments which are most crucial to the organism, for which there are enough data to permit extrapolative projection. City planning wants to anticipate the general socioeconomic situation and specific governmental actions significantly affecting the municipal population, revenues, or operations. Similarly, to the extent feasible, corporate planning observes economic, financial, monetary, technological, organized labor, and other trends which affect its profits and prospects.

Military planners project the size and composition of the military forces of potential adversaries, and follow established procedures of detecting hostile intentions before they are translated into military action. Changing conditions or circumstances may add or subtract from the environmental projections which should be made, but a set of impactful externalities for comprehensive planning remain constant.

Some projections can be numerically calculated: such as those for many physical substances, engineering systems, accounting data, population growth, or the destructive effects of explosive weapons. They may be precise within a probable percentage accuracy, or the projection may be made for a range between upper and lower limits. The validity or degree of accuracy of the projection may depend on some single or several factors: birth and mortality rates in population projection, interest rates and the borrowing capacity of businesses, or down-time for the maintenance, repair, and operational availability of weapons systems. Inaccuracy or a change in the value of such key factors can significantly modify or invalidate the projection.

> A high degree of accuracy is possible. . . in predicting the future age composition of the population [in the United States]. . . . Almost all the people who will be alive in the near future have already been born. To obtain reliable estimates you need only apply the appropriate mortality rates, which are very predictable, to each of the various age groups (or "cohorts") and add them up. And if we are focusing on the population over 10 years old, no estimates about birth rates are needed to project 10 years out. (Freund)

Theoretically, for greatest accuracy the projection of separate elements should be quantitatively and mathematically integrated into one multiple projection for the organism as a whole. But there are so many elements and aspects which should be taken into consideration that this cannot be done with present analytical knowledge. Except for the simplest organisms, the best that can be done is to calculate the interrelationships among as many of the most important primary elements as feasible. The remainder must be taken into account judgmentally.

Projection is applied to both natural and human change. As noted earlier, the predictability of natural changes varies widely. Since human change is planned and undertaken to achieve a definite objective, the projections involved should be sufficiently reliable to make the attainment of the desired objective highly probable. Deliberate action toward a predetermined end is normally limited to what can be reliably projected. Human change with a low probability of success is more an intentional gamble than a carefully devised plan. Emergencies are a special situation in which something must be done, however blindly.

Context. . . .
3. Associated surroundings, whether material or
mental. . . .

(*Webster's New International Dictionary of the English
Language,* Second Edition (Unabridged), 1960, Vol. I,
p. 576)

Open-End. . . .
1. Having no definite limit of duration or
amount. . . .

(*Webster's New Collegiate Dictionary,* 1977, p. 245)

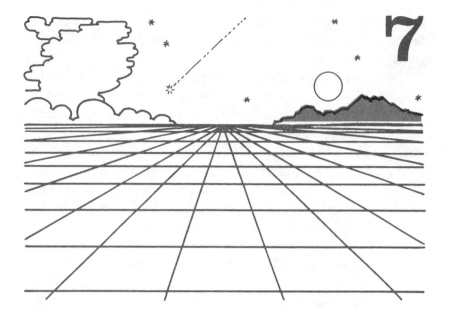

THE OPEN-END CONTEXT
OF PLANNING
Potential Pitfall

WE KNOW FROM HUMAN KNOWLEDGE accumulated throughout history—particularly that acquired during the past century or so—that all organisms interact through the incredibly complex totality of physical and biological interconnections which constitute the inanimate and animate world. Every element of every organism relates in some way with every element of all other organisms: directly and immediately, or remotely through a long chain of interconnections over a long period of time. Human beings can comprehend only a small number of these infinite interrelationships, and reliably project into the future only a tiny fraction of them. People can therefore successfully manipulate relatively few of their current activities and only a minute part of the total global environment.

By definition and intent, comprehensive planning is the intellectual field and practicing profession that is committed to view situations more broadly than any other. It is natural therefore for comprehensive planners to note the external interconnections as well as the internal dynamics affecting the organism with which they are concerned. They know that no human organism exists in a vacuum but within an immediate environment on which it depends in many ways. They are keenly aware that governmental entities and business enterprises are tied together in a worldwide web of spatial, economic, political, social, technical, and other interrelationships; that military planning is interconnected with the existing and potential capabilities of potential adversaries separately and in different combinations. And that these extensive interconnections relate to global geologic, geographic, and meteorologic events which in turn are affected by galactic forces.

Naturally, comprehensive planners would like to comprehend and incorporate the effects of all these externalities in a logically complete analysis of the organism being planned. But they realize that the first tier of immediate interconnections is linked with a second tier of close interrelationships, a third tier somewhat indirectly, and so on to the earth as a whole and the universe beyond. In this sense, the context of planning is open-ended. Theoretically, all identifiable interconnections should be considered; but this is impossible intellectually and practically. There is neither the knowledge, time, nor money to even attempt to encompass analytically the range and sequence of identifiable interconnections. Despite this apparent fact, experience indicates that the absence of boundaries to comprehensive planning constitutes a potential intellectual and procedural pitfall which can impair or eliminate its effectiveness.

Since by its nature comprehensive planning is fraught with uncertainties, there is a natural tendency for the planner to seek assurance through thorough study. Furthermore, the conclusion reached and the staff recommendation he or she makes to the decision-maker would most likely be correct if they were based on analytical study that is complete in every respect. At the least this would protect the planners from the claim that they have not considered some aspect believed to be important by a concerned individual or group. This is most apparent in connection with environmental impact reports, which are frequently challenged by opponents because the impact of the proposed activity on one or more of the thousands of organisms affected in some way is not incorporated in the report. Or military planners may be induced to add more and more desirable features to a proposed weapons system until it becomes too complex for effective use in the battlefield and prohibitively costly. Conceptual entrapment by the open-end context of planning rarely occurs in corporate business planning because the pressures of the market place and the necessity of making a profit preclude any serious attempt to seek a complete analytically-proven best solution.

Searching for the analytically complete solution can not only delay vital decisions beyond the time when they are still applicable, but vitiate the usefulness of the planning process itself. This attempt can be the inadvertent consequence of a sincere but mistaken effort to know all, or a deliberate tactical device to avoid reaching a conclusion. Returning a matter to an individual or committee "for further study" is a procedural move employed by humankind since earliest times to delay or prevent consideration or resolution of the matter, without any formal indication that this is the intention.

Effective comprehensive planning requires recognition that all elements and aspects of whatever is being considered can never be completely covered analytically. Successful application of the planning process in human affairs does not depend on total knowledge any more than it does for other human endeavors. It does, however, emphasize the importance of selecting those primary elements for analytical consideration that are most representative of the functioning and future of the organism. This is especially true for these elements that will most affect its longer-range future. Since only so many elements can be analyzed at one time in the Representation of the Entirety described in the next section, it is important that those chosen are the ones that simulate the organism most closely. The impossibility of complete analysis also emphasizes the necessity of always thinking in terms of probabilities. There is no absolute certainty, only relative uncertainty.

The illusion that somehow comprehensive planning can encompass the open-end context of planning and thereby assure a successful future for human organisms also tends to overcentralization. More and more planners are added gradually to central staff to assume responsibilities previously performed at divisional, departmental, or other subordinate levels of the organization. When this occurs, effective planning of the organism is impaired: either because of duplication or conflict between the analyses conducted separately by central and component planning staffs; or because central staff operates under the illusion that it is analytically possible and managerially feasible for it to perform both comprehensive planning for the organism as a whole and operational and functional planning for its component parts.

Representation. . . .
1. Act or instance of representing (in various senses); state of being represented; exhibition; symbolization; substitution; also simulation.
2. A likeness, picture, model, image or other reproduction. . . .

Represent. . . .
1. To bring clearly before the mind; to cause to be known, felt, or apprehended. . . .
2. To present by means of something standing in the place of; to exhibit or to be the counterpart or image of, to typify. . . .

Entirety. . . .
State of being entire; entireness; also, that which is entire; a whole; sum total. . . .
Entire. . . .
1.a. Complete in all its parts. . . .

(*Webster's New International Dictionary of the English Language,* Second Edition (Unabridged), 1960, Vol. II, p. 2114; Vol. I, p. 854)

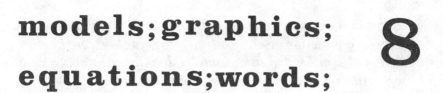

models;graphics;
equations;words;
data;models;graphics;
equations;words;data;
models;graphics;equa
tions;words;data;mod

8

REPRESENTATION OF
THE ENTIRETY
Basic Reference

PLANNING REQUIRES SOME ANALYTICAL representation of the organism being planned. The organism itself cannot be manipulated for planning purposes: either because of its nature, the irreversible effects of such manipulation, operating requirements, or excessive cost. The extreme example is the use of self-destructive testing when the physical behavior of the object cannot be predetermined from a small-scale model, mathematical abstraction, or some other simulation. The purpose of planning, of course, is to determine in advance, not to discover after the fact that unintended changes in the organism have been brought about by the process of predetermination itself. *Unless the organism can be conceived and expressed in some usefully descriptive or analytically representative way, it cannot be planned effectively.*

Forms of Representation

The required representation can take many forms, depending on the type of organism and activity. Primitive man undoubtedly traced out on bare ground a rough diagram of some physical arrangement or perhaps a plan of attack on an enemy position. A model of a steam device is described by Hero of Alexandria early in the second century A.D. The technically innovative and anatomically explanatory drawings of Leonardo da Vinci are representations of entireties in two-dimensional form on paper. Subsequent development of perspective drawing advanced the portrayal of three dimensions on a flat surface. Some representative object, graphic formulation, physical model, or other descriptive indication must accompany every patent application. Every plan of a building or structure is a representation of the final product.

Today, models are used for many simulative purposes. Both small-scale and full-size models are part of designing automobiles, aircraft, satellites, ships, and a multitude of simpler industrial products: often tested in wind tunnel, artificial weather chamber, hydrodynamic water tank, or on a shake-table to predetermine their performance under anticipated environmental conditions. Miniature replicas of machinery and equipment are sold commercially for the scale models used by industrial engineers to study alternative layouts for manufacturing plants. Scale models of harbors, estuaries, and portions of river systems with mechanically created water flow, wave action, and tides are used in designing ocean and river installations. The flight simulators that are used regularly to check out commercial airline pilots on emergency procedures in case of fire, stall, engine failure, and other malfunction are so realistic in terms of movement, sight, sound, and smell that the pilots react physically and emotionally as they do under real crisis conditions.

Similarly, abstract representations have been conceived by humankind since the beginning: mental simplifications of real life phenomena, abstract concepts, or imaginary picturizations within the human brain. Their expression as symbols on paper constitutes most of intellectual knowledge, and their translation into patterns of action accounts for most of political and military history. An accumulation of hundreds of thousands of abstract mathematical and other symbolic formulations describe forces, conditions, and interrelationships of matter in physics, chemistry, and biology. Accounting systems are accepted simulations of the operations of a business. Scientifically selected statistical samples—comprising as small a fraction of the total population as is necessary for the desired reliability of results—are commonplace in interim national censuses, opinion surveys, product quality control, and other research directed at a distinct group of people, quantity of objects, or commercial market.

If the concept of representation is extended further, literature and fine arts symbolize in their particular way subtle, complex, unquantifiable aspects of the human condition and aesthetic environment. The extent to which outstanding conceptual and literary masterpieces serve a representative purpose is exemplified in the vast reference made in the Western world to the Bible, works of Shakespeare, and the Constitution of the United States, or in widespread reaction to the Mona Lisa and Beethoven symphonies. Precisely what literary works and fine arts represent for different individuals can only be stated from their subjective viewpoints; but the successful simulation of feelings and attitudes by these works is evident by the breadth and depth of their impact. Any one of the many forms of representation may be employed in planning a particular element or activity, but certain of them are most useful in comprehensive planning for the organism as a whole.

Internalized Simulation

First and foremost are the simulative images that are formulated in the mind of the planning analyst and decision-maker. All matters that an individual absorbs, reviews, or decides are internalized in the mind and memory as accumulated observations, experience, formal knowledge, and thought. This accumulation includes highly specific and clear concepts, partly formulated thoughts, vague images and impressions, and sensory inputs that are not consciously noted. Pictorial memories, visual constructs, assorted data, correlations, judgments, intuitions, and feelings are all present—well ordered, confused, or in process of development as the case may be. Mental awareness is broad and can shift rapidly between diverse subject matter and numerous considerations. Some of the mentally stored material is remembered immediately, some requires deliberate recall. No inanimate device can approach an equal range of sensory input and cognitive interconnection. It is this internal representation that is the foremost evaluative reference for the planning analyst and decision-maker. Although intuitions are part of reasoning and serve certain planning purposes particularly well, unrecognized or unheeded emotional blocks or biases can impair the rational thought that is the principal means of planning comprehensively.

Established Methods

Supplementing and extending the internalized representation of each decision-maker are the various methods developed over the centuries to present the information needed for planning analysis and to portray the results of this analysis. Graphics are probably the most ancient and certainly the most widely used and comprehended of these methods. Diagrams, bar charts, trend lines, curves depicting data, maps, plans, and abstract delineations of situations and ideas are familiar examples. In recent years their formulation has been both speeded up and extended by computer graphics. Various forms of statistical statement are available; and reduced-scale physical models of structures and forces have long been at hand.

Mathematical Models

Since early times geometry has provided the mathematical representations that engineers need to design many kinds of military and civil structures. Throughout the years the primary purpose of applied mathematics has been to simulate a great variety of situations and interrelationships. Utilizing the high-speed calculation, memory capacities, and manipulative capabilities of electronic computers, mathematical models are widely employed in both basic research and current operations. Operational uses by civil government, business, and the military services include payroll and general accounting, inventory control, various forms of production scheduling. In business, mathematical models also make possible worldwide aircraft and hotel reservation systems, the efficient routing of long distance telephone calls, or optimum product marketing and distribution plans. The military employ them for logistic supply purposes, keeping track of all orbiting vehicles and debris, and aircraft and ship location. Governments use them for population and other quantitative projections. Mathematical models also correlate the diverse inputs involved in gaming developed to simulate civil governmental, tactical military, and competitive business situations for the edification and education of their respective or prospective participants.

Specialists in the Defense Department and in the field commands, try to anticipate situations in which the antagonists and their weapons are known. They have concocted immensely detailed scenarios. . . . Some studies, plans, and net assessments are the raw material for tests by the Studies, Analysis & Gaming Agency. There, another small staff of officers with wide operational experience and specialized skills in operations research, computers, and political science or economics use computers to put simulated conflicts through their paces. (Halloran)

There are examples of successful mathematical modeling of activities which can be quantified and mathematically correlated and projected with the required numerical precision. They may comprise a single element or component of the organism, or a subsystem composed of several organizationally distinct but closely interrelated activities. Usually, they simulate operational activities rather than strategic matters, tangible rather than intangible elements, short-term rather than long-term considerations. Although they are formulated in mathematical terms, human judgment can be incorporated at particular points in the mathematical model and calculative process. Some relatively simple organisms can be successfully directed for all practical intents and purposes by mathematical models that accurately represent the crucial operational components and their interactions.

Mathematical models are part of comprehensive planning for most of the large complex organisms which constitute the mainstream of human activities and most vitally affect the future of humankind.

[Their] components are variables, factors that characterize the situation—a business, a market, an industry, a national economy. . . . Each model tries not only to include all necessary variables, but to accurately represent their relationship one to another. Thus, by changing a variable . . . policy makers can see what happens to the system as a whole. (Zarnowitz)

For many years, smaller businesses have been managed successfully as represented by operating and profit-and-loss statements and balance sheet, despite the important elements that are not included in this accounting combination. In corporate planning today, this information and additional data concerning cash flow, inventory, production costs, interest and foreign exchange rates, for example, are maintained in a computerized statistical-mathematical model simulating the financial condition of the company. In the combat information centers of aircraft carriers, or in those on land for the intercontinental ballistic missile system or the worldwide fleet of nuclear submarines, computerized mathematical models keep track of fast-changing facts and figures relating to the military situation and command decisions. Mobile command posts are being tested by the U.S. Army: equipped with small computers which record, store, correlate, and display the reported disposition, strength, and movement of friendly and hostile forces within the area of military operations—the kind of "representation of the entirety" useful for army field commanders. In civil government, the broadest use of mathematical models at the federal level is probably by the Office of Management and Budget and the Congressional Budget Office because of the enormous number of interconnected quantities they must consider. State and local governments also maintain econometric and other kinds of mathematical models for various purposes. Computerized econometric models are required to optimize the financing of new towns, with their large "front-end" costs and long-delayed monetary return.

Comprehensive Representation

In each of the above examples, the mathematical model is only one part of the representation of the organism required for effective comprehensive planning. It expresses only those elements that can be quantified and manipulated mathematically. And there are, of course, many additional elements and considerations which must be stated in non-numerical form and taken into account by non-mathematical analytical methods: such as policies, goals, political factors, human actions and reactions, hostile or competitive intentions, legal aspects, administrative organization, means of implementation—to name but a few. During World War II, the underground command center established in London to coordinate the defense of Britain against invasion by Germany incorporated as many operational elements as could be handled simultaneously at that time. Today, the Situation Room in the White House or the briefing room of the U.S. Joint Chiefs of Staff are probably the closest approximations of the kind of comprehensive representation of the entirety needed for strategic military planning and decision-making. Both corporate and city planning centers that comprise a comprehensive representation of a business or municipality have been proposed but not yet implemented in the United States (Branch, 1962, 1981). These would include: historical references, statistical compilations, graphical formulations, mathematical models and other abstractions, legal materials, statements of planning goals and policies, designated planning objectives and programs of effectuation, political and environmental considerations, the results of validating the comprehensive representation. Establishment of the "fourth power" of government referred to earlier in this volume would constitute a comprehensive representation of the federal entirety.

The following features should be incorporated in every analytical representation established for comprehensive planning purposes. It must maintain information depicting the primary elements most closely indicative of the functioning of the organism, whether or not they are quantifiable. This information must be accurate enough to reflect the activity or condition it

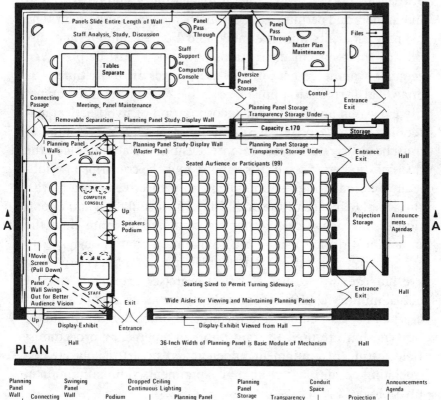

PLAN

Panels Slide Entire Length of Wall
Panel Pass Through
Panel Pass Through
Master Plan Maintenance
Files
Staff Analysis, Study, Discussion
Staff Support or Computer Console
Tables Separate
Oversize Panel Storage
Control
Entrance Exit
Connecting Passage
Meetings, Panel Maintenance
Planning Panel Storage Transparency Storage Under
Capacity c.170
Storage
Removable Separation
Planning Panel Study-Display Wall
Entrance Exit
Hall
Planning Panel Walls
STAFF
Planning Panel Study-Display Wall (Master Plan)
Planning Panel Storage Transparency Storage Under
or
COMPUTER CONSOLE
Seated Audience or Participants (99)
Entrance Exit
Hall
Up
Speakers
Podium
Projection Storage
Announce-ments Agendas
Movie Screen (Pull Down)
Panel Wall Swings Out for Better Audience Vision
STAFF
Exit
Seating Sized to Permit Turning Sideways
Entrance Exit
Hall
Up
Display-Exhibit
Entrance
Wide Aisles for Viewing and Maintaining Planning Panels
Display-Exhibit Viewed from Hall
Hall
36-Inch Width of Planning Panel is Basic Module of Mechanism
Hall

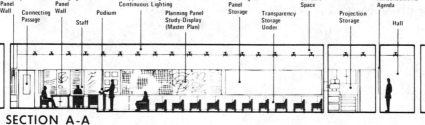

SECTION A-A

Planning Panel Wall
Connecting Passage
Swinging Panel Wall
Staff
Podium
Dropped Ceiling Continuous Lighting
Planning Panel Study-Display (Master Plan)
Planning Panel Storage
Transparency Storage Under
Conduit Space
Projection Storage
Announcements Agenda
Hall

**REPRESENTATION OF A CIVIL GOVERNMENTAL ENTIRETY
CITY PLANNING CENTER**

represents with sufficient reliability for the planning purposes involved. To the extent possible, information should be expressed in numbers and permit statistical-mathematical comparison. The primary elements must be integrated by determining and displaying their current interactions. And they must be projected separately and together into different stages of future time. The analytical formulation must be flexible enough to allow immediate revision and permit the incorporation of hypothetical material simulating different situations. The total representation must be clearly portrayed, comprehensible and acceptable to the decision-makers it serves. Its validity must be confirmed periodically by comparing its simulative and projective accuracy with the actual behavior of the organism. The installation and operation of the analytical mechanism cannot cost more than the organism it depicts can afford to maintain continuously.

Some representations that simulate part of a larger organism are full-size: war games and fleet exercises employing troops, actual military equipment, and ships; the mock cockpits of aircraft and space vehicles and the navigation bridges of oil supertankers that are used to train pilots in emergency procedures; field testing of equipment under actual or artificially created operating conditions; or animal experiments simulating human physiology.

Continuous. . . .
1. Having continuity of parts; without break,
cessation, or interruption; without intervening space
or time; uninterrupted; unbroken; continued; as a
continuous road or murmur.
2. Operated without interruption; as a continuous
report. . . .

Process. . . .
1. Act of proceeding; continued forward movement;
procedure; progress; advance. . . .
2. A course of procedure; something that occurs in
a series or actions or events. . . .
4.a. Any phenomenon which shows a continuous
change in time, whether slow or rapid; as the *processes* of nature; the *process* of growth; a mental
process. **b.** A series of actions, motions, or operations definitely conducing to an end, whether
voluntary or involuntary; progressive act or trans-
action; continuous operation or treatment, esp. in
manufacture; as, the *process* of vegetation or
decomposition; a chemical *process*; a *process* of
reasoning; a *process* of making steel. . . .

(*Webster's New International Dictionary of the English
Language,* Second Edition (Unabridged), 1960, Vol. II,
p. 1972)

CONTINUOUS PROCESS
Planning and Plans

IN THE MOST FUNDAMENTAL and universal sense, organisms never cease to function entirely. Some form of internal activity continues whether the animate organism is in a state of operational inactivity, abandonment, bankruptcy, truce, hibernation, or metamorphosis. And the external environment affecting the organism is never constant. The basic energy of the organism continues in a different form or state even in animate death and inanimate material transformation.

Therefore, comprehensive planning for continuously functioning organisms cannot be successful if it is applied sporadically or only at regular intervals. Internal conditions can develop,

133

external events can occur, or the environment can change: requiring immediate modification or complete revision of current
plans. Under adverse circumstances, failure to respond quickly
can be seriously damaging or fatal. No planning can be so completely and accurately conceived that it covers all possible contingencies and could not benefit from some adjustment or potential improvement perceived during the period of acceptance
and implementation. Sometimes it may not be cost-effective to
make the change, but the constant awareness that identified the
possible change will lead to adjustments in planning which are
worthwhile under a different situation of cost and benefit. The
comprehensive planning process, like the learning process in
general, should therefore be applied continuously.

Many planners tend to use the terms *planning* and *plans*
interchangeably, despite the fact that they are not the same. In
comprehensive plann*ing* particularly, it is important to differentiate between the two terms. *Planning is the active process of
continuously formulating what the organism is able and intends
to carry out with respect to its future, and how it expects to do
this.* Plans, on the other hand, indicate the actions to be taken
during a prescribed period of time to achieve specific objectives.
Metaphorically speaking, comprehensive planning is the continuously "moving picture" of the organism, composed of a
succession of plans analogous to the individual "picture frames"
of a moving picture. The integration inherent in planning produces a synergistic capability greater than the sum of the capability of the component parts, which are distinct organizationally,
analyzed individually as well as collectively, and implemented
separately.

The attainment of a predetermined end requires a plan formulating the substance and sequence of the separate actions
which must be taken. Plans symbolize resolution of the many
considerations involved which could be studied and debated
interminably, and they provide the operational and programmatic specificity required for effectuation. They are part of the

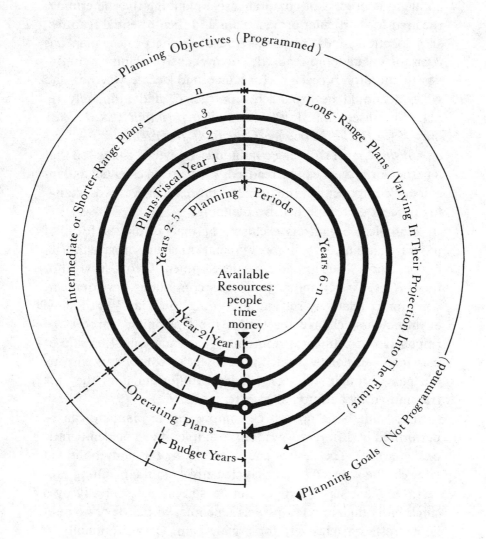

**CONCEPTUALIZATION OF THE
CITY PLANNING PROCESS**

Melville C. Branch, *Continuous City Planning, Integrating City Planning and Municipal Management,* New York (John Wiley & Sons), 1981, p. 97. Reproduced by permission.

continuous process of comprehensive planning that determines the need for particular project plans and their essential features, size, location, and financing. And after the project plan has been formulated and realized, comprehensive planning continues to monitor project performance and decide whether and when it should be expanded, contracted, and ultimately replaced or discontinued. *Plans—explicit or implicit as the case may be—are the instruments required for predetermined accomplishment:* of stopping continuous analytical change so that a particular project can be realized. They are an essential and inevitable component of the broader, more inclusive, ever-changing process of comprehensive planning.

Biological organisms exclusive of man display a form of natural planning in their always remarkable and often astonishing behavior. Their progressive development favors survival of the species. At certain stages in this continuous development, behavior is relatively set and according to "plan" until some environmental change reactivates the "planning" process of responsive adjustment or mutation. The same might be said of inanimate substances, which are subject to continuous entropy but pass through states of relative equilibrium until they are transmuted by an internal or external force.

The same basic process of comprehensive planning can be performed in different ways. For example, it can be democratic or dictatorial. The desires and decisions of the body politic at large can be induced to participate actively in the planning process. Or planning objectives can be determined centrally by a single individual or a few powerful people, with little or no public interest or exclusively for private gain. Organizationally, it can be highly centralized or decentralized to the extent possible. It can be quick-acting to serve a fast-changing organism or to respond to emergency or unexpected situations. When warranted and feasible, it can be deliberate and prolonged to minimize risks. Dependent on the organism being planned and the information available, the analytical content and the process of planning may be quantitative, technical, computerized, and automated; or it may be primarily judgmental and intuitive. Certainly, the way comprehensive planning is organized and conducted is the most important determinant of its success.

A plan is successful if its end product serves the intended purpose, it is completed on schedule, and requires no more resources than were estimated and allocated at the beginning. Care must be exercised when costs and time of completion are deliberately underestimated, as they often are for example with weapon system projects in the United States: in competition with the other military services, or to secure initial congressional approval with the expectation that once the commitment is made cost overruns and schedule extensions cannot be denied. In corporate and civil comprehensive planning there is the troublesome habit of subordinate units overstating costs and budget requests to compensate for the routine reductions regularly made by higher authority. Plans can be evaluated by their product or performance only when they are reliably costed, and completed before extraneous factors interrupt or nullify the programmed effectuation.

Evaluating comprehensive planning is even more difficult than judging its component plans. By definition as well as in practice it covers many more elements and considerations, including those that are too intangible or indefinite to be incorporated in specific project plans. Comprehensive planning is subject to frequent adjustment and revision. It does not have the fixed beginning, specific program of accomplishment, and completion date of project plans, but functions continuously with many diverse inputs and contributions. It is therefore difficult and often impossible: to identify cause and effect in comprehensive planning; to trace its proposals and their exclusive consequences over an extended period of time; to attribute positive results among the planning staff, operating units, and chief executives; and identify changes in the planning process brought about by independent externalities and random chance. For these reasons, there are only several methods of evaluating comprehensive planning and these are almost entirely judgmental in nature: a record or log of achievements claimed by the comprehensive planning staff which can be confirmed, denied, or modified by the decision-makers involved in its activities; the observations and conclusions of a committee of independent and qualified persons specifically selected to evaluate the planning effort; and the comprehensive planning director's evaluation of his own and his staff's performance. All three together would be worthwhile if continuation of the comprehensive planning activity were in question. (Branch, 1981)

There are countless plans when they are defined as broadly and fundamentally as they are in this book. They range from the minuscule to plans global in scope, involving collectively the full range of existing knowledge. One type of plan programs a series of actions which experience demonstrates have a high probability of producing the desired result. An example is a plan to transfer a business, civil governmental, or military unit from one place to another.

> "The Vatican Collections: The Papacy and Art". . . may well be the most expensive art exhibition to organize and ship on record. To put it together . . . took diplomacy and logistical planning that would have impressed even Napoleon. (Saltzman)

Experience indicates that such a move can be planned with near certainty, although it is known that minor modification of the move plan will probably be required because of some unforeseen happening, and a catastrophic event could possibly postpone the move or require its complete revision. Complex architectural and engineering plans and specifications belong to this category because they also are composed of elements, actions, and projections that can be extrapolated and carried out with considerable certainty, as demonstrated by myriad examples throughout history.

A second general category of plans has less specific, more comprehensive, and longer-range objectives, involving in corporate planning:

Trends which are not yet discernible, circumstances which have not yet crystallized, events which have not yet occurred, decisions which have not yet been reached. Areas in which such assumptions may be necessary include general and particular economic conditions, government policy, rates of technological change, product demand and market potential, and competitive achievements. (Woolridge)

The outcome of plans of this type is far less certain than the outcome of plans consisting of predictable actions to achieve limited objectives that can be conceived and projected precisely beforehand. Plans that are more comprehensive require continuous application of the best analytical capability, the greatest built-in flexibility, and the wisest decision-making. It is this type of plan that is formally adopted by governmental, business, and military organizations as part of continuous planning, employing such descriptive adjectives as: comprehensive, master, general, developmental, system, corporate, business, war, or military operation.

Project plans are of course enormously diverse. Some are short-term, modest, utilizing few resources. Others are long-term, ambitious, requiring a substantial share of the discretionary resources available to the organism. They may involve a single function, a subsystem of closely related activities, or all of the primary elements of the organism. They may call for a simple program of effectuation, or an intricate sequence of steps necessary to attain the desired results. The end-product may be a physical structure, an advancement of human capabilities, or a different organizational arrangement. The probability of success and expected rewards may be high or low. Some plans, such as the move plan referred to above, may consist of a precise schedule of programmed actions to attain a clearly defined end-product. Others formulate a set of uncertain or alternative accomplishments whose exact content and sequence will be determined as implementation proceeds. Many of the different kinds of plans may be involved in the comprehensive planning process at the same time.

Plans represent the conscious intentions and actions of humans, and the evolutionary equivalent in other animate organisms. Their content ranges across the entire spectrum of human knowledge and endeavor, and the entire accumulation of genetic forces.

Feedback. . . .
1.a. The return of a portion of the output of any process or system to the input, especially when used to maintain the output within predetermined limits. **b.** The portion of the output so returned. **c.** Control of a system or process by such means. . . .
2. Broadly, any information about the result of a process.

(William Morris, Editor, *The American Heritage Dictionary of the English Language,* 1971, p. 482)

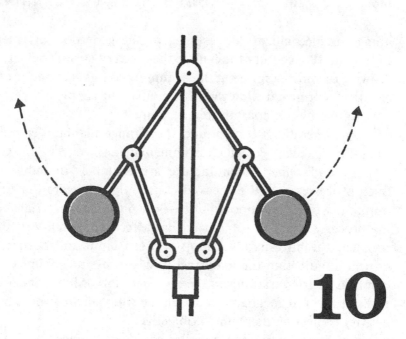

FEEDBACK

Interrelating Plans and Performance

OR SOME SEVERAL HUNDRED million years animate organisms have responded to the felt consequences of their movements by adjusting their behavior in the slow but continual process of evolutionary development. The animate world today is the product of this reactive process. The involuntary and voluntary feedback involved in human actions is exemplified in the first instance by the automatic response of the pupil of the eye to the intensity of light or the heartbeat to exertion, and in the second case by the constant adjustment of our physical movements to our visual and tactile intentions as we proceed with our activities. Feedback is also incorporated in numerous mechanical devices such as the governor, invented during the 18th century to regulate the speed of steam engines, a drawing of which appears at the beginning of this section, or the electrical thermostat widely used to control the supply of heat or cold to maintain a constant temperature.

Some operations control and short-range planning employ "real-time" feedback, which is immediate and continuous. Oil refining and cement manufacture are examples in industry. Such processes must be checked constantly to ensure that the output is what it is supposed to be. When the raw materials being processed vary in some way that affects the quality of the product, the informational loop between input and output is critical in adjusting the manufacturing process to minimize or compensate for variations in the raw materials. All quality control is a form of feedback to determine whether the productive activity is meeting its planned objective.

In military operations, missiles could not be accurately directed between moving platforms and moving targets without the almost instantaneous feedback provided by electromagnetic or acoustic sensing systems. Successful command and planning of ground warfare depends on the feedback of intelligence in the battlefield concerning hostile military movements.

In civil governmental operations and planning, the supply of electricity and water are linked in a reciprocal relationship with industrial, residential, and agricultural demand, with their adjustment particularly important during peak periods of use. Police tactics vary with information fed back from central computers concerning the vehicle or person under observation.

If comprehensive planning is to be effective, it must not only operate without interruption as described in the previous section, but it must also be able to check continually the consequences of its policies, projections, and plans. When it is determined that these are not working out as intended, adjustments can be made. Feedback can also identify the early stages of un-expected trends, events, or aggravated conditions which require alteration in planning. Other things being equal, this reduces "government by crisis" with its unfortunate consequences.

Feedback in comprehensive planning requires establishing a system of monitoring, reporting, and observing that is percep-tively and reliably responsive. It cannot provide the rigorous application of feedback that closely measures the interrelation-ship between specific forces or activities and their output or consequences. There are too many diverse elements and aspects involved in comprehensive planning for such analytical preci-sion. Rather than the direct, immediate, measurable, and un-mistakable interaction between cause and effect illustrated by a thermostat, feedback in comprehensive planning is general, inexact, and not mathematically calculable. But it is more ap-plicable and valuable for overall directive purposes because it is not restricted to the narrow content required for scientific accuracy.

Not all feedback needs to be immediate and continuous, as is necessary for some industrial processes. In most manufactur-ing, periodic sampling provides sufficient quality control. Close correlation of input and output to meet established standards or to achieve immediate results is a form of extremely short-range planning more commonly referred to as operations control. If adjusted and revised at very short intervals, planning becomes synonymous with operations control. Under whatever nomen-clature, continuous reading of results and instantaneous direc-tive reaction tends to obscure consideration of the general strategic situation, longer-range trends, and related elements that are a vital part of comprehensive planning which normally occurs before the activities it considers are undertaken.

It requires time to incorporate new information into ongo-ing analysis, to study longer-range trends, identify the primary elements involved, reach conclusions, and initiate plans incorporating changes in operations. Close and continuing feedback is therefore more often justified in operations control than comprehensive planning. In local governmental planning, for example, elected decision-makers might like continual feedback concerning public opinion. With the utter conviction that re-election is their public duty as well as their private and personal interest, politicians are willing and able to fine-tune their directive reactions and legislative actions to the electoral mood of the moment, or to whatever supports them politically. Were such continuous political feedback incorporated in the comprehensive planning process, it would benefit the self-interest of elected decision-makers but not the organism they are obligated to serve.

The need for immediate and continuous feedback varies with different organisms, the kind of comprehensive planning conducted, internal operating conditions, the external environmental situation, and special circumstances. For example, business normally requires faster feedback of the consequences of corporate planning than civil governments and the military services which can take longer to plan—except in times of civil emergencies, imminent hostilities, and war. Ordinarily, the conscious planning of human activities requires more rapid response concerning results than other biological organisms which can take very long times adjusting to environmental change.

Organisms whose continuous planning does not respond promptly to sudden changes in the socioeconomic or physical environment occurring within the area of their activity, cannot compete successfully with other organisms whose internal operations permit prompt feedback. Emergency situations demand immediate reaction, and their consequences usually require changes in the longer-range, strategic aspects of comprehensive planning. Natural catastrophes of fire, flood, earthquake, explosion, pestilence, and pollution call for the immediate response of civil authorities over communication systems designated for this purpose. Urban and regional planners sometimes forget that state and local governments compete with each other for commercial business, industry, tourism, tax revenues, monetary grants, and in many other ways. Failure to plan promptly to meet competition results in comparative disadvantage. The plans of military establishments are competitive responses to the military capabilities of potential adversaries: requiring far faster or immediate feedback of military intelligence during war than for anticipatory strategic planning.

Naturally, areas of social and environmental sensitivity are observed more continually than those demonstrating relative stability. By their nature some elements of comprehensive planning are subject to more rapid change: the weather, economic conditions, certain public attitudes, international monetary exchange rates, the precise disposition of military forces. Other elements of comprehensive planning can be projected with considerable accuracy during the normal intervals between the gathering and feedback of information: such as population growth and composition, land use, housing, business competition, environmental conditions, or military capabilities. Annual estimates suffice for many planning purposes.

Experience gained during the planning and implementation of project plans and at other times can be applied to comparable efforts whenever the lessons learned are relevant—and provided they are recalled. This is why the accumulation, continuity, and availability of planning experience and knowledge are so important. This longer-range intermittent form of feedback can be effected within each organization, at public libraries or other depositories, or in a governmental institution such as the "fourth power" referred to in Chapter Two.

Some feedback involves data which must be kept consistent over time to permit continuing statistical comparison. Other correlations are derived from general observation, random inquiry, and subjective judgment, which are no less significant because they cannot be accurately quantified. The expense of maintaining current information, including feedback, is an important consideration in comprehensive planning. The cost depends on many factors. Accurate projection can reduce the need for feedback as one element of this expense by providing the interim information which would otherwise have to be more frequently collected at additional cost.

Uncertainty. . . .
1. Quality or state of being uncertain. . . .
Uncertain. . . .
1. Indeterminate as to time, number, amount, extent, etc. . . . .
2. Not certain to occur; subject to accident, chance, or change; indefinite; problematical. . . .
3. Not certain or reliable; untrustworthy as a course or agent. . . .
4.a. Not known beyond doubt; dubious. . . . **b.** Not clearly assured; doubtful. . . . **d.** Not clearly identified, defined.
5. Not definitely directed; undecided. . . .
6. Not constant; changeable; unsteady; variable; fitfull. . . .

Risk. . . .
1. Hazard; danger; peril; exposure to loss, injury, disadvantage, or destruction. . . .

Ambiguity. . . .
2. Ambiguousness. . . .
Ambiguous. . . .
1. Doubtful or uncertain, esp. from obscurity or indistinction; also, inexplicable.
2. Capable of being understood in either of two or more possible senses; equivocal. . . .
3. Capable of classification in either of two or more categories. . . .
4. Uncertain as regards course or outcome; problematic in tendency.

(*Webster's New International Dictionary of the English Language,* Second Edition (Unabridged), Vol II, pp. 2761, 2154; Vol. I, p. 81)

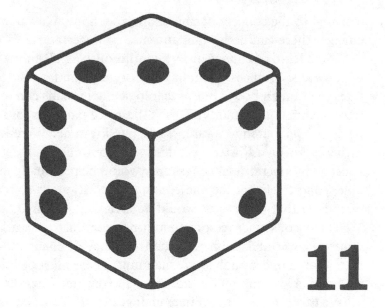

11

UNCERTAINTY, RISK, AND AMBIGUITY

Constant Condition

Uncertainty

THERE IS, OF COURSE, no absolute certainty. No one knows for sure that the sun will shine tomorrow, despite its long history and predicted future, each extending over billions of years. However high the probability that the sun will indeed rise tomorrow and life on earth continue to exist for a very long time to come, *humankind exists in an environment of total uncertainty: of continuous change and relative probabilities without exception.* Change and the possibility of change are

151

essential to the concept of uncertainty; without an awareness of change, there can be no human sense of uncertainty.

Some form of change occurs continuously in all animate and inanimate substances, including the organic matter that constitutes the human body. But psychologically humans can tolerate only so much uncertainty. This is the price paid for consciousness: people's unique awareness of passing time. Were human activities to be adjusted ceaselessly to continuous change, the consequent operational uncertainty would be personally intolerable, collectively unacceptable, and organizationally so severely disruptive that operations would be seriously impaired.

These consequences of attempting to adjust to continuous uncertainty establish limits to the frequency of change that can be tolerated in comprehensive planning. There must be intervals of relative certainty and stability. Favorable times must be selected to propose and initiate changes from the usual and the accepted. People must be motivated or willing to adjust to needed or desirable change. Effectuation of any project or activity requires a progressive reduction of operational uncertainty and managerial changeability as it proceeds from commencement to completion. Otherwise nothing would ever be finally finished. The most effective planning follows a progression of diminishing increments of change: each representing achievements or modifications smaller and smaller in size that optimize the outcome and do not disrupt, needlessly prolong, or prevent completion of the project or program. These are examples of operational aspects of uncertainty to be considered in comprehensive planning.

Two kinds of uncertainty are involved in planning. One relates to changes constantly occurring in the biological and physical world over which humans have little or no control: ocean tides; global weather; earthquakes; geochemical, electromagnetic, and other physical forces. The second type includes the very wide range of natural forces and events that humankind can affect in some measurable or observable way by their activities or attitudes: natural selection by modifying the environment; regional weather by cloud seeding; waterways by dams, levees, and other engineering works; or large surface areas by massive earth movement and environmental degradation. Of course, humans shape the social, political, legal, monetary, financial, cultural, and other activities which they formulate and conduct. However fixed and institutionalized these activities, they can be changed if people decide to do so.

The first of the above categories can be called the uncertainty of natural forces and events; the second the uncertainty of human actions and activites. In both cases, when enough comparable experience or specific observation has accumulated to link cause and effect, event and results, situation and consequences, *judgmental probabilities can be formulated and exercised.* They may represent personal intuition or logical induction, or they may result from one of the myriad social, political, economic, fraternal, and other organizations created over the years which produce judgments or stimulate their formulation. Groups can also be scientifically structured to produce collective expert opinion.

When the number and comparability of repetitive occurrences are large enough, and numerical data concerning the interrelation of cause and effect are available, *mathematical probabilities can be calculated.* Their extensive use today in industrialized societies is well established: in insurance, scientific sample surveys, weather forecasts, target accuracies of military weapons, the physical behavior or material substances, sports performance and tactics, and many other applications.

In comprehensive planning, probabilities may be employed to reveal statistical interrelationships, unexplained correlations between events and consequences, uniform trends, curves of likely development, or repetitive fluctuations. But this is possible only for those elements that can be expressed in numbers

and treated mathematically. Relatively few of these are among
the primary considerations normally involved in overall comprehensive planning for most organisms. And the numerical
specificity required for the calculation of probabilities must be
worth the time and cost it requires. This is why the continuous
observation of trends noted under Projection, Principle 6, and
the Representation of the Entirety, Principle 8, are so important
since they are the best mechanisms of predictive judgment when
mathematical probabilities cannot be calculated. Tolerance and
Flexibility, Principle 12, are specific allowances for uncertainty.
And Natural, Human, and Purposive Change, Principle 3, are
sources of uncertainty which in most instances cannot be calculated mathematically.

There is always the temptation in human affairs to seek the
imaginary comfort of absolute certainty. The degree of assurance desired or required affects almost every aspect of human
organizations: the cost of comprehensive planning, the method
and level of confidence of decision-making, the probability of
decisions being correct, the extent and pace of operational commitment, willingness to risk, or vulnerability to serious setback.
Inattention to the risk posed by uncertainties invites failure, for
there is always the risk of doing nothing. Overprotective attempts to cover and minimize every risk can bankrupt and stul-
tify the organism.

Risk

Risk is the relationship of uncertainty to hazards and other
conditions significantly affecting the functioning of animate
organisms: all of which are subject to some degree of risk because of the universality of change and the consequent uncer-
tainness it inevitably creates. Comprehensive planning must be
concerned with changes and uncertainties which present a hazardous or milder form of risk for the organism.

There are voluntary and involuntary risks: the first illustrated by driving an automobile, crossing a traffic way, or any

one of the dozens of chances people take every day; the second by the hazards presented by every electrical distribution system or by nuclear radiation from an unknown source. Besides the perils presented by "acts of God" and the natural and man-made hazards covered by insurance, there are risks that affect the functioning of the organism in a much less catastrophic, severe, or direct way. For example, whenever alternative management decisions are possible—and this is almost always the case—there is the operational risk of making the wrong choice. Even the use of data often involves a risk as to its reliability and applicability. The consequences of such operational risks may be minor or major, immediate or long delayed, subtle and gradual rather than catastrophic. Under certain circumstances, a low-level management decision can lead to business failure, or a tactical mistake by a junior officer can escalate into a major military defeat. Some risks are individual in that they are taken by and mainly affect one person, others are collective or societal when numbers of people accept or are subject to the risk. The two are linked, of course, since comparable individual cases can aggregate into groups of people or an entire society.

The attitude of people toward risks varies greatly: with different individuals, cultures, religions, and circumstances. The cautious person of wealth will insure himself against more perils than a person inured to the restricted choices of poverty. More fatalistic cultures accept greater risks. And avoiding the risk of eternal damnation is an important motivational force for the firm religious believer. The person wanting to die for his or her country or for another cause welcomes endangerment. In general, people want to minimize risks which threaten their self-interest, welfare, safety, and above all their survival.

In civil governmental planning, potential hazards are the reason for traffic regulations, health and sanitation, building and safety, and zoning codes, environmental standards, flood plain insurance, agricultural price supports, rules regulating occupational hazards in the workplace, and many others. In business, risk is taken into account in many ways: insurance, provision of financial reserves, cash flow analysis, market testing of proposed products, alternate sources of supply, cost-plus contracts. The military services seek to reduce the momentous hazards of war by preparing plans to cover various contingencies, accumulating enough military force to make victory highly probable, providing reserves and avenues of retreat for specific operations, by military intelligence and surveillance of hostile intentions to reduce the chance of surprise, or by weaponry and tactics designed to reduce one's own casualties and maximize those of the enemy.

Comprehensive planning cannot possibly take into account all the uncertainties and attendant risks affecting most organisms. Only the more important of these can be considered. In general, the hazards presented by the natural world are easier to treat than operational or societal risks. The level of risk that is safe enough is a matter of judgment: supported by calculations of the consequences of the catastrophe, adverse event, or negative development; and estimates of the cost of eliminating or reducing the risk. The costs of the adverse consequences and the cost of mitigating the risk are the two sides of the cost-benefit equation. "Risk-benefit analysis" or "risk assessment" is done regularly by business and civil government to decide the advisability of insurance covering risks to property and people. Similarly, the military services develop important information for planning purposes by comparing the benefits to be derived from the potentially destructive effects of enemy weapons with the cost of counteracting them.

The hardest hazards to evaluate are those that have widespread effects and are difficult or impossible to measure, aggregate, and compare numerically: air, water, and biological pollution, toxic and nuclear waste disposal, infectious disease. It would be helpful in planning to be able to compare the costs of introducing and the value of the expected benefits of new technologies, proposed regulatory measures, and new management procedures that are not hazards in the usual sense of the word, but nonetheless are definite risks because their success is by no means assured. A number of relationships have been established which affect risk management generally. As would be expected, acceptance of risks relates to the benefits to be derived; people are much less willing to accept involuntary than voluntary risks; the rate of death from disease appears to relate to people's acceptance of voluntary risk (Starr). At present, quantification of operational and societal risks requires determining in each case whether precise numbers can be developed that are reliably descriptive rather than misleading. Structured judgment is as important as mathematical computation and comparison of risk probabilities.

> The *estimation* of risk is a scientific question. . . . The *acceptability* of a given level of risk, however, is a political question, to be determined in the political arena. (Handler)

> There is need to measure societal risk more accurately . . . ; to determine the level of expenditure for risk reduction beyond which adverse economic and political effects may be overriding. . . . (Okrent)

In civil governmental planning there is the constant political pressure of special interests to reduce the particular risk with which they are concerned. The military services seek overwhelming superiority to reduce the possibility of war, military defeat, or heavy casualties. In corporate planning, each unit manager wants to reduce any risks that threaten the profits of the organizational component for which he or she is responsible.

Ambiguity

Ambiguity is uncertainty caused by lack of clarity or precision. Sometimes, particularly in the political arena, ambiguity is deliberately created to obfuscate, confuse, or to avoid commitment until attitudes and reactions have been expressed. Sometimes it is the result of negligence, lack of knowledge, insufficient investigation, or unwillingness to take the time to be precise and unambiguous. Almost always, this produces persistent problems: years of litigation in the case of carelessly written legislation, managerial confusion or indecision in the case of corporate planning. In military affairs, ambiguity can be fatal. Sometimes, clarification of ambiguity is expected to be worked out gradually over time: by a process of acceptance and rejection, progressively proposed resolution, tentative action and reaction, trial and error, or eventual decision by higher authority. Some subjects such as the specification of environmental impact regulations are best clarified gradually because it is undesirable or impossible to define them specifically at the outset.

Unless ambiguity is introduced or retained for some special reason, deliberate or inadvertent indefiniteness is incompatible with comprehensive planning, which is intended to transform uncertainties, possibilities, and probabilities into plans and programs of action. It is important, therefore, to note any ambiguities involved in the analytical and decision-making process and to clarify them as soon as possible. Otherwise, the unresolved subjects or questions they represent cannot be considered in the judgmental or logical process of comprehensive planning, much less included in quantitative data and mathematical analysis. As they are defined in the first chapter, planning objectives cannot be formulated when ambiguities prevent the programmatic specificity these objectives incorporate. If ambiguities are replaced by alternatives, they remain indefinite only to the extent of the choices presented. It is normal in comprehensive planning for some activities to await resolution of relevant ambiguities which cannot be resolved immediately. But if these ambiguities are important, there is unwanted and disruptive delay; if they are crucial, the entire process of comprehensive planning must await their resolution.

Tolerance. . . .
3. A specified allowance for error in weighing,
measuring, etc., or for variations from the standard
or give dimensions, weight, or the like. . . .

Flexibility. . . . State or quality of being flexible;
flexibleness; adaptability. . . .
Flexible. . . .
4. Responsive to, or readily adjustable to meet the
requirements of, changing conditions; as, a flexible
scheme of government. . . .

(*Webster's New International Dictionary of the English
Language,* Second Edition (Unabridged), 1960, Vol. II,
p. 2661; Vol. I, p. 966)

TOLERANCE AND FLEXIBILITY
Accommodating Change

AS NOTED IN PREVIOUS sections in various connections, comprehensive planning operates in the real world which is forever changing. Natural and human change are involved constantly as indicated under Principle 3. And as explained under Principle 9, it must function as a continuous process adjusting to this inevitable change, avoiding the conceptual, analytical, and procedural rigidity that ensures failure. *One way that comprehensive planning provides for change is by incorporating tolerance and flexibility in the continuous process of planning, in plans intended to attain particular results, and in specific programs of accomplishment.*

Tolerance is allowance for expected, probable, or possible error. Either exact calculation is analytically impossible or impractical, or some critical element of the analysis cannot be closely calculated but only estimated within a range of accuracy. Tolerance is also provision for the variation to be expected in the behavior of materials and the performance of products. We live in a world of countless materials and objects, each with elastic, electromagnetic, and other physical properties which limit their successful functioning. The known limits established for these properties by scientific test or comparative calculation are taken into account in product and project planning.

Most human activities also have tolerances: limits beyond which they cannot vary without significantly altering the nature and prospects of the operation, or requiring its revision. For example: traffic lanes provide enough additional space on each side of the average size automobile to allow for normal variations in steering; aircraft are supplied with a fuel reserve sufficient to allow reaching an alternate airport; a floating zone is approved in a proposed urban development project to allow a particular land use to be located anywhere within a specified area as the final project design is worked out. Or in a purely socioeconomic plan such as a rent supplement program, eligibility is defined flexibly enough to include all those entitled to participate but not specifically identified in the legislation. In military activities, tolerance is provision for expected losses of personnel and equipment, the known range of accuracy of weapons, or allowable variation in designated tactics or strategy.

Flexibility is the capability of adjusting to more diverse conditions and unexpected developments. It is more broadly responsive than tolerance. Whereas tolerance pertains most often to a limited range of probable error or physical variation in different components of an organism, flexibility applies to its functioning as a complete entity. Thus, when operations are no longer possible within the limits of tolerance, flexibility allows for the substitution of another material or a different mode of operation. Flexibility provides for the response to change of complete organisms: consisting of parts which function separately each within its tolerance limits, and others with a broader built-in adaptability. Flexibility means the possibility of choosing among several alternative policies and plans, being able to substantially revise a comprehensive plan without vitiating past attainments or jeopardizing intended accomplishments.

It is the nature and range of their potential adjustments to change that differentiate tolerance and flexibility. Tolerance provides for expected variation. Flexibility allows compensative adjustment for possible and improbable developments, and a range of completely unexpected occurrences. The U.S. intercontinental ballistic missile (ICBM) system illustrates this difference and at the same time the far-reaching consequences of military decision-making involving the two concepts of change. Many factors combine to produce the average error or "bias" between the target and impact points of a ballistic missile. This target error—or tolerance—of individual missiles is of primary importance in designing an ICBM system which produces offensively the desired destructive effect on the enemy, but is also flexible enough to minimize the destructive effects of a hostile ICBM preemptive strike. This flexibility has been achieved in one way by placing missiles aboard a fleet of nuclear-powered submarines whose whereabouts are unknown because they are constantly moving around the oceans submerged in an unpredictable pattern. Comparable flexibility on land was the purpose of the system proposed in 1980: to consist of 4,600 ICBM launching sites in the far west of the United States, among which 200 missiles would be moved about secretly in a complex, costly, and continuing version of the age-old "shell game."

The decision to build the MX missile and to spend billions to hide it from a surprise Soviet attack [flexibility] is

perhaps the most visible and costly consequence of
the narrow interpretation of the consequences of Soviet
missile accuracy [tolerance]. (Smith, 1982)

Flexibility has many different forms. For example electronic
mechanisms optimize the capacity of transcontinental communications systems by assigning long distance telephone calls to
routes that are underutilized at the moment. The design of
buildings can make their internal rearrangement relatively easy
or prohibitive. At an urban scale, the overall flexibility of traffic
movement on a freeway system focusing radial routes through a
single central point downtown is greatly increased by the incorporation of circumferential connection toward the periphery.
At a regional scale, the transmission lines of different producers
of electricity are interconnected in a combined grid system
allowing the interchange of electricity between component units
when one subsystem fails. Policies can provide flexibility:

> States and industries will be allowed greater flexibility in
> regulating air pollution under an Environmental Protec-
> tion Agency policy. The expanded "bubble policy" will
> allow a company that reduces or limits its emissions to
> trade or sell credits to another company in the same area
> that is violating clean air standards or wants to widen its
> operation. (*The Wall Street Journal,* April 1982)

The type and extent of flexibility vary with different stages
of comprehensive planning. At the earliest stage, alternative
policies and directions of desired development are formulated
for the organism as a whole. As the time for action arrives, one
of the alternatives is selected and its implementation begun.
Flexibility is retained within the different components of the alternative selected until their prospective effectuation requires
commitment. As smaller and smaller units or activities are involved in the progressive sequence of effectuation, flexibility is
more and more limited. This occurs with respect to the organism

as a whole and each of its components until implementation is accomplished. Because development is not uniform throughout the organism, various stages of flexibility are being applied to its different parts at any one time.

The normal need for adjustment is precluded when planning is conceived as a series of fixed end-state plans as noted in the section on Objectives, Principle 4. The comprehensive planning process must be flexible enough to adjust to changing circumstances, and react immediately to unexpected events as often as need be. The primary requirement is to identify, analyze, and act upon the usual situations that call for progressive action to avoid their becoming major problems. When crisis conditions are allowed to develop or unexpected emergencies arise, flexibility can accomplish less because fewer options are available at these times. Normally, opportunities for constructive advancement far outnumber emergency situations; the forethought they require constitutes the steady change and improvement that characterizes sound comprehensive planning. Among the many matters to be considered is determining when to improve or replace what currently exists, one of the most difficult analytical problems in comprehensive planning: typified in industry by the continuing question of when to replace existing machinery and modify present manufacturing processes; in civil government by how often to change laws and regulations; and in the military services by the development of new weapons systems. Such decisions require sound judgment based on careful cost-benefit and cost-effective analyses.

The axioms concerning change that are propounded with respect to human affairs generally apply also to comprehensive planning. The correct timing of decisions initiating change is important: neither before nor after they should be made. Options are incorporated in planning to provide flexibility; they are retained as long as they are useful, to be replaced by new alternatives associated with the option that was exercised. Provision of a reserve or "cushion" of financial and other resources allows activities that cannot be abandoned immediately to be phased out while new ones are realized. A strategic or tactical fall-back position permits adjustments that might be impossible without this leeway. Unalterable long-range commitments are rarely desirable: the longer they are retained without modification after inevitable change has rendered them inefficient or ineffective compared to feasible alternatives, the more costly the waste of resources and the greater the adverse effects upon the organism.

Peak. . . .

3. The topmost point; the summit; as the *peak* of happiness; spec., the highest point in a course, development, or the like, esp. as represented by a graph; as, employment is at a *peak;* the peak of the demand.

4. The maximum point of a load curve, as of a load-time curve of a power station.

5. *Com.* The highest point to which prices rise in a given period.

6. *Elec.* The maximum value of an alternating quantity during a cycle. . . .

(*Webster's New International Dictionary of the English Language,* Second Edition (Unabridged), 1960, Vol. II, p. 1798)

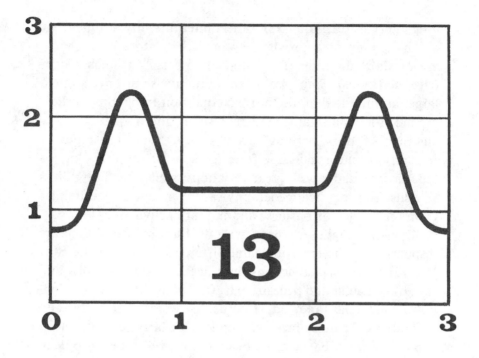

PEAK PERIODS

Planning for Peak Loads

PEAK PERIODS ARE PARTICULAR forms of change involving above average activity and stress: almost as universal as the change involved in tolerance and flexibility discussed in the previous section. But they are sufficiently distinct to merit separate identification and treatment. If extremes of temperature, precipitation, insolation, and other environmental effects are regarded as peak periods, most animate and many inanimate organisms experience such occasions.

The physical world exhibits a wide variety of peak periods of many kinds: storms, floods, fires, earthquakes, heat waves, freezes, droughts. Some of these occur randomly at short or long intervals (earthquakes), others intermittently at times that can be closely or approximately predicted (monsoons). Some are of short duration (flash floods), others last much longer (riverine floods). Some are much more intense or have a much larger amplitude than the normal condition (typhoons), others are much less unusual (thundershowers). The frequency of occurrence of peak periods varies widely. Some are repeated regularly in much the same form (seasons of the year), others reoccur irregularly with great variation (tsunamis). These illustrations from physical geography can be matched by examples from the worlds of business and military activities.

Day and night are peak periods for organisms that are responsive to the environmental differences between the two. Everyday human activity involves peak periods of work and rest, of vehicular and pedestrian traffic, of agricultural, residential, commercial, and industrial use of water, electricity, and natural gas. Families face peak periods of birth, death, illness, and other stress. Farmers are busiest at harvest times, people in retail business at Christmas and other holiday periods, winter and summer resort operators at the relevant seasons with favorable weather, military personnel during peacetime maneuvers and wartime combat, civil governments in emergencies.

During peak periods organisms are under exceptional stress and require more energy or the application of more resources than at other times. This poses an important question for comprehensive planning. If it is decided to accommodate the maximum possible peak load regardless of how greatly it exceeds the average condition, there is substantial excess capacity most of the time. A disproportionate share of available resources is almost always required to meet the exceptional situation which occurs occasionally and often unexpectedly.

The systems of major automobile thoroughfares in cities are an example. Were they designed and built to accommodate the heaviest traffic peaks during the early morning and early evening rush hours, they would be two-thirds underused during the rest of the day and night. It has been said that if the capacity of existing major highway systems in cities were doubled or even tripled, they would immediately be filled to capacity at peak periods by those waiting for the reduced congestion that exists briefly after additional highway capacity is constructed. If the system were planned to also accommodate without increased congestion the traffic generated by large crowds attending for several hours occasional events at a few stadiums and auditoriums, excess capacity during normal times would be even greater.

Some human organisms cannot even consider meeting brief periods of maximum demand because the added direct and indirect costs equal or exceed the income or other benefit derived. Although the unit cost of meeting peak demand may be less for some activities, total cost is always greater. Certain ways of meeting peak load situations can be unproductive or destructive: cutthroat price wars; bureaucratic competition for directive control of governmental assistance to communities during civil disasters; progressive escalation of the nuclear forces of the great powers to meet the projected or presumed peak provisions of each other.

When the peak load represents a condition that must be met at all costs, the necessary resources must be allocated or obtained if the organism is to function and survive. Thus, the heat-resistant covering of a space plane must prevent its destruction during reentry through the earth's atmosphere. Offshore oil-drilling rigs must be built to withstand the fiercest weather reported in the past plus a further safety factor. A community confronted with a near certainty of catastrophic inundation at some indefinite future date must install flood control for its self-preservation. Municipal building and safety codes require that the design of buildings support the live load projected for the structure. A seasonal business faced for a short time each year with a large cash flow drain must accumulate the necessary cash reserve from its own operations or secure short-term loans in order to survive this period. Wars are also characterized by critical peak periods—some anticipated, others not—which must be surmounted somehow to avoid defeat:

> Large construction is coming . . . in 1941, but the crisis will be reached long before 1941. . . . I am beginning to feel very hopeful about the war if we can get round the next three or four months. . . . the loss of destroyers by air attack may well be so serious as to break down our defense of the food and trade routes across the Atlantic. (Churchill)

In her own subtle and effective way, nature has taken peak loads into account in the evolutionary process, by building up internal adjustments to peak periods of environmental change, and by the various responses of animate life to cyclical overpopulation. Human organisms respond to expected peak loads by organizing themselves accordingly. An example of successful organization to meet unpredictable demand—referred to in the section on Feedback—is point-of-sale recording, overnight re-ordering, immediate manufacture and rapid delivery arranged to "ride the curve" of temporary impulse buying. To the extent possible, the military services are obligated to plan for the "worst case" or peak load of hostile confrontation.

Most human organisms do not attempt to meet the maximum possible peak periods and loads that they experience. They find it to their advantage to plan to support only the average demand or need. Consumers, customers, and voters accept the fact that the peak periods they prefer cannot or will not be served as successfully as at other times, and adjust their activities accordingly.

In business, excess capacity created by peak loads can be eliminated or reduced by product diversification or by the addition of services that even out activity over time. Peak periods can also be met by cooperative planning: such as the pooling of firefighting, police, public health, and other personnel and equipment from different governmental jurisdictions during civil emergencies; or the regional interconnections between separate utility systems that enable excess capacity in one location to be used in another location experiencing a peak load at the same time. This kind of cooperation among private enterprises is limited in the United States by antitrust laws. *It is a task of comprehensive planning to analyze how peak periods and peak loads are best handled by the organism involved.*

Some peak periods are beneficial in whole or in part. In various parts of the world, flood tides cleanse harbors which otherwise are stagnant or become polluted. For thousands of years the annual inundation of lands along the Nile River in Egypt supported agriculture for the population. Whether the new irrigation system inaugurated upon completion of the Aswan Dam will be successful as planned remains to be seen. Despite the damage they cause by flooding, monsoons are critical to agricultural production in lands around the Indian Ocean and Southeast Asia.

Comprehensive planning cannot regularly provide for catastrophes. Rarely are the resources available to human organisms enough to compensate for the destructive effects of the worst possible peak situation. Nor is it feasible for most organisms to retain sufficient resources in reserve for peak periods so severe that they occur very infrequently and unpredictably. It is normally preferable to apply available resources to providing adequately for average everyday requirements. In most cases, the resources available are barely sufficient to meet these average needs and the moderate peak periods characteristic of so many organisms.

Time. . . .
1. The period during which an action, process, condition, or the like continues. . . .
2. The point or period when something occurs, the moment of an event, process, etc. . . . .
3. The allotted, appointed, fixed, or customary moment or hour for something to happen, begin, or end. . . .
4. Fitting moment; proper or due season; favorable opportunity. . . .

Priority. . . .
1. Quality or state of being prior, or antecedent in time. . . .
3. An order that takes priority over all others. . . .

Sequence. . . .
1. State or fact of being sequent; a following or coming after or in succession.
2. A series having continuity and connection. . . .
4. The quality of having orderly, esp. logical, connectedness of successive events or parts. . . .
5. The order in which events are connected or related in time; simple succession; esp. the connection of antecedent and consequent in temporal series, apart from causal necessity. . . .

(*Webster's New International Dictionary of the English Language,* Second Edition, (Unabridged), Vol. II, pp. 2648, 1968, 2283)

TIME AND PRIORITY

Sequence

THE TIME REQUIRED IN nature for events to occur or
tendencies to develop independently without deliberate
human intervention varies widely: from the seismic shock
of an earthquake lasting seconds to the years required under ordinary conditions for serious soil erosion and loss of fertile top-
soil; from the immediate reaction of biological organisms to
environmental changes beyond their threshold of tolerance to
almost imperceptible evolutionary adjustments brought about
over many hundreds of thousands of years; from short-range
shifts in human attitudes to long-range persistence of basic
motivations.

Most people are aware of the tremendous variations in the size, complexity, and time required to plan and realize the multitude of projects and diverse endeavors undertaken by man. The Panama and Suez Canals, Tennessee Valley Authority, Alaskan Oil Pipeline, a new model aircraft or large industrial plant, equal voting rights and fair employment practices, and numerous military weapons systems illustrate large-scale projects involving many years from commencement to completion. Planned endeavors of modest size are legion: the many projects families undertake, moderate improvements in small business practice, small-scale military tactics, civil governmental services, or any one of myriad activities requiring relatively little time to conceive and implement.

Timing is a necessary consideration in planning. Certain endeavors must occur at the right time because they either depend on or support other activities with which they are linked operationally. These interconnections may have to do with materials, money, people, production, environment, or any of the different elements and activities of an organism that constitute its functional existence. Most often they must occur in a certain sequence. The timing of another category of planning endeavors depends on situational rather than operational conditions. For example, planning proposals that are not feasible in a depressed economy, in times of exceptional social stress, or when politics are unfavorable, may be appropriate and well received at a more propitious time. Sometimes proper timing may depend on a very specific situation: such as the opposition or support of a single individual, passage of legislation, even favorable astrological or other mystical signs in more instances than decision-makers care to admit.

Any one of these interconnections can change overnight: perhaps requiring immediate adjustment in the planning of the specific project or activity involved, and possibly corresponding modification in the planning of the higher-level organism of which the project or endeavor is part. Or changes may occur very slowly permitting such extensive alterations as a revision of the methods employed in planning analysis, adoption of different policies, or complete reprogramming of actions and activities. Reaction to unexpected developments can lead to the planning process being shortened, lengthened, speeded up or slowed down, temporarily halted, or abandoned.

Consideration of a time span of past, present, and future is of the essence in comprehensive planning. This raises important questions which must be resolved. How much reliance can be placed on past experience to indicate what is likely to occur in similar situations today? Are informational data for past periods sufficiently reliable and numerically comparable to provide a statistical base for projections into the future to be used in planning? What is the best balance between stable intervals and periods of planned change that avoid the developmental disadvantages of too long a time with little or no change, and the operational disruption of too frequent and rapid change? How far into the future should comprehensive plans extend: fewer years with greater certainty, or for a longer span with less assurance? The answers to such questions differ drastically with different organisms, different objectives, available resources, external environmental conditions, and according to a host of specific situations, circumstances, and events. It is the analytical purpose and responsibility of comprehensive planning to recommend optimal answers to these basic questions.

The conduct of comprehensive planning involves time in other ways. If the process is to have the flexibility deemed essential under Principle 12, it must allow rapid modification of data and analysis, and their complete revision within the interval of time appropriate for the organism. On the other hand, as the time for transforming plans into actions or objects approaches, changes become more difficult, disruptive, costly, and ultimately impossible if there is to be an actual outcome or result. The relative importance of time is clearly greater in an emergency situation demanding immediate response than during normal times. Productivity is not necessarily increased in direct proportion to the reduction in the time it takes to perform an activity because the human and material resources needed to achieve this reduction are part of the measurement of productivity. Time can also be employed competitively, aggressively, punitively, and destructively as well as constructively.

Limitations and requirements of time, as well as the relative functional importance of the elements constituting the organism, establish priorities at various levels of organization and activity. By definition, comprehensive planning by top management must consider or at least be aware of as many of the most significant elements and aspects of the organism as feasible. Since all of these components cannot be analyzed thoroughly, continuously, and flexibly at the same time or in the time normally available, as noted in Section 5, effective analysis of the most crucial of them must be assured by some form of integration discussed under Principle 5. There is rarely enough time— not to mention insufficient knowledge and inadequate budgets—for comprehensive planning to do more than treat the primary components. Nor would trying to "do everything" be constructive for Principle 7 indicates the futility of pursuing the open-ended context of planning. And the Representation of the Entirety, Principle 8, can encompass analytically only the most significant of the elements and considerations involved in sizeable human organisms.

Priorities are an essential part of comprehensive planning since they establish the necessary and desirable sequence of its actions and activities. They vary in importance over time and under different circumstances. What may be relatively inconsequential at one point in time may suddenly become preeminent. A single event can bring about drastic change. As one illustration, in early 1982 few could have foreseen that overnight the Falkland/Malvina Islands would become the number one priority of England's military and political planning. Compared with other issues, consideration of environmental impacts was a low priority in U.S. urban regional planning until the passage of environmental legislation in the early 1970s applying to the activities of first federal and then state governments, and subsequently to private development projects requiring some governmental approval. In private enterprise, specific priorities in comprehensive business planning may be altered by depressed sales, changes in interest of foreign exchange rates, a new or competitive product, labor strife, politics and governmental regulation, or any one of numerous happenings.

Contingent and absolute priorities are two of the kind of priorities involved in planning. Contingent priorities are those that are flexibly interrelated but not mutually interdependent. They can affect each other in different ways that change within a range of time. Priorities in the political, social, and economic aspects of comprehensive planning belong in this category because the issues and objectives involved do not ordinarily require an exact sequence of effectuation, each complete within a given interval of time. Also, policies do not involve programming because they are general goals to be attained by whatever means and opportunities arise. Policies and planning activities relating to broad issues need not be made specific and prioritized until they are formulated into planning objectives which by definition incorporate an indication of the precise means and methods of their accomplishment.

Certain planned activities require absolute priorities and programming. The steps or stages involved follow a strict sequence, each one completed or partially completed before the next one begins, each assigned a prescribed time for completion. All actions and activities are closely correlated, programmed, and scheduled sequentially or in parallel. Construction projects and assembly line operations are familiar examples. The foundations and utility connections underneath a building must be completed before construction of the superstructure they will support is begun. The different parts of a product manufactured on an assembly line are put together in a precise order and with a time allotted to each step; several subsystems may be produced in parallel at the same time and combined in a final assembly. Military plans for an amphibious landing on hostile territory program precisely the necessary sequence of offensive operations: neutralization of coastal defenses; landing of troops, weapons, and supply vehicles; winning the battle; provision of combat replacements and reserves; and ultimately the establishment of occupation forces. Cash flow management by business or government requires exact programming of expenditures and receipts, production levels, inventories, and other factors affecting the flow of funds into and out of the organism, so as to minimize or eliminate the cost of short-term borrowing to cover peak periods of disbursement when cash reserves are low. Techniques developed specifically for programming include several graphical methods, Program Review and Evaluation Technique (PERT), and the Critical Path Method (CPM).

Summarizing, time is an intrinsic part of all activity. Planning seeks to affect the future by present actions. It requires choosing and establishing a priority of primary goals, policies, and objectives: taking into account their relative significance for the organism, resource requirements, and operational characteristics. By definition, the statement of planning objectives incorporates how they will be achieved: the sequence and timing of successive actions and activities—subject to modification, revision, or abandonment as dictated by circumstance. There are three general phases in the comprehensive planning process: variously labeled strategic or developmental; tactical, operational, or current; implementation or effectuation. They are all, however, part of a process that is never-ending in time and continuous in its consideration of the past, present, and future, short-range and long-range, broad and specific.

Jurisdiction. . . .
1. Law. The legal power, right, or authority to hear and determine a cause, or causes, considered either in general or with reference to a particular matter; legal power to interpret and administer the law in the premises. The jurisdictions of different courts. . . .
2. Authority of a sovereign power to govern or legislate; power or right to exercise authority; control. Sphere of authority; the limits, or territory, within which any particular power may be exercised. . . .

Area. . . .
4. A particular extent of surface; a space on the surface, as of an organism; a region; specif., a tract of the earth's surface. . . .

Coverage. . . .
1. Act or fact of including or covering; condition of being covered; an aggregate of items covered. . . .

Scope. . . .
4.b. Space for freedom of movement; room; range. . . .
6.a. Range or extent of view, intent, or mental activity. . . .
b. The range within which an activity displays itself. . .; also, the field to which a subject is limited. . . .

(*Webster's New International Dictionary of the English Language,* Second Edition (Unabridged), 1960, Vol. I, pp. 1347, 145, 613; Vol. II, p. 2241)

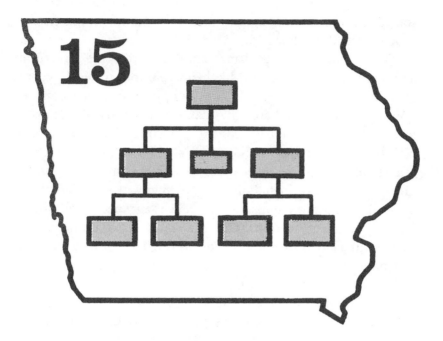

JURISDICTION, SCOPE, AND AREAL COVERAGE

Determinant Considerations

COMPREHENSIVE PLANNING and decision-making by human organisms are limited to their legal jurisdiction, organizational scope, or areal coverage: separately or in combination. A city council cannot make decisions that are binding upon other levels of government or beyond its municipal boundaries. Executives of one private enterprise are not empowered to make decisions for another business entity. A commanding officer issues orders only to the military unit he commands, and each military service only to its own personnel unless there is a unified command. And within each civil governmental, business, and military organism, the respective spheres of decision and areas of activity of their administrative subdivisions are delineated.

Other biological organisms function within the structural and spatial limits established by their evolutionary development over the ages. Insect societies, for example, adjust their population size to the ground area they can cover for sustenance or to meet some other areal determinant. They may found new colonies, transporting their spatial domain with them when they migrate to another area. Territoriality is firmly established in most individual animals, including humans: many of which combine as families, kinship groups, or interdependent species with a collective areal identification. Plant life reacts to and influences its surrounding environment in various ways. The constituent parts of plants expand, contract, bend, or stiffen in space depending on temperature and moisture content. Root systems extend a limited distance from the plant stem, and leaves, needles, pollen, and other organic materials are transported from the plant to the surrounding area by wind, water and other environmental and topographic forces.

Inanimate materials also affect their immediate surroundings in various inorganic and often predictable ways: expansion, contraction, gravitational pressure, heat, chemistry, electromagnetism. Radioactive and toxic substances are conspicuous examples. Even an inanimate material as relatively fixed and immutable as steel exists within the domain of its inorganic effects, however microscopic they may be.

Comprehensive planning by every human organism functions according to some implicit or explicit jurisdictional, organizational, or areal scope. Its exact arrangement is determined by precisely how it is conceived and conducted, but successful comprehensive planning exhibits certain common organizational characteristics. The chief decision-makers of the organism to which it is applied recognize that the overwhelming operational demands upon their time and attention, characteristic of their position, preclude their producing by themselves the analysis needed for comprehensive planning. This supportive analysis is conducted by an individual or group of people attached organizationally to the office of the decision-maker who makes the crucial decisions and issues the order and instructions; it is conducted as the decision-maker desires and directs. Care is taken that the results and recommendations of this comprehensive planning analysis are passed on directly and exclusively to the chief executive, and not prematurely by staff to subordinate line managers thereby impairing both the jurisdictional prerogatives of subordinate managers and the authority of the chief executive and primary decision-maker. Comprehensive planning does not occur when the topmost decision-makers do not believe they need or benefit from analytical support, or are unable or unwilling to use and organize it effectively once it is established. In small organizations, the comprehensive planning process is basically no different because it is conducted entirely in the head of the chief executive.

Although comprehensive planning may affect organisms other than the one for which it is intended, through numerous simultaneous effects or by the progressive impact of fewer effects, it can directly determine or command only those activities that fall within its jurisdiction or scope. Extensive human activities are subdivided into distinct administrative units to facilitate or make possible effective management of the organism as a whole. Each of these organizational units is associated with an area or region representing its administrative jurisdiction. Designation of these functional and areal subdivisions is as diverse as the kinds and forms of human activity they represent. They may be demographic, geographic, regulatory, operational, political, or military in nature. They may relate to sales, manufacturing, distribution, of some other functional activity. The range of organizational purposes and designations is vast.

Existing jurisdictions rooted in history, custom, or law affect whether and how comprehensive planning can be accomplished. A widely recognized example involves the continuous

built-up expanse of almost every metropolitan urban area in the
United States: composed of many separate municipal jurisdictions and numerous special purpose districts each covering a different area, their boundaries indistinguishable on the ground.
But they all share common problems and requirements: transportation, land use, water supply, energy, sewerage, flood
control, waste disposal, environmental pollution, protection of
persons and property. This has created the need for overall metropolitan planning and at the same time made its realization
difficult or impossible because of people's emotional identification with the municipality in which they live, and their reluctance to relinquish real or imagined "home rule" in any way.

In corporate planning, time and a careful strategy of actions
are required to change long-established managerial jurisdictions
represented in the corporate organization chart; executives adversely affected by proposed readjustments resist them energeti-
cally. In military planning, after many years of acknowledged
need, jurisdictional competition still prevents effective comprehensive planning of the unified operations of the four military
services:

> The uniformed head of our armed forces is not a person
> but a committee. . . . They have a built-in conflict of in-
> terest. Even in the [Joint Chiefs of Staff] conference
> room . . . they inevitably work for the bureaucratic in-
> terests of their respective services, and not for the collec-
> tive armed forces. . . . What the country has long need-
> ed is a unified general staff not answerable to the Army,
> Navy and Air Force bureaucracies, and with a single uni-
> formed individual in charge, under the Secretary of De-
> fense. . . . The Soviets have a unified general staff. So
> do the Germans (at last), the French, the Canadians and
> the British. (Kester)

Unresolved jurisdictional problems and disputes can of
course prevent all sorts of comprehensive planning. At a global

scale, planning mechanisms have yet to be developed to resolve acid rain and other environmental pollution problems between Canada and New England in North America, between Sweden and Norway and the Low Countries in Europe, and elsewhere in the world. The respective responsibilities and accountability of the U.S. federal and state governments are a matter of continual contention and random resolution. As yet, there is neither the political means nor an analytically defensible method of establishing fiscal and operational responsibility for economic needs, social deterioration, environmental pollution, and other problems that extend across different jurisdictional boundaries. Parochial concerns and jurisdictional limitations make it increasingly difficult—if not impossible—to plan comprehensively to avoid the crisis conditions brought on more frequently as crucial problems of society are no longer localized but are regional, national, and global in nature and scope.

The way in which the activities of the organism are to be conducted determines how it will be organized administratively and areally, the extent of managerial decentralization, the assignment of different directive responsibilities, and the number of component units that must be integrated. Other considerations aside, the more numerous the decentralized units, the more difficult it is to coordinate their different activities. The more centralized the management, the greater the informational and analytical demands upon the comprehensive planning staff to develop the required data, determine the needs, and formulate planning objectives for all units of the organism. The larger and more complex the organization, the broader and more strategic the comprehensive planning at the top: setting goals, establishing policies, and defining general objectives for the primary units of the organism which transform them into planning objectives by determining specifically how they will be achieved. However, as indicated elsewhere in this book, strategic considerations in comprehensive planning should never preclude early identification of particular developments or small-scale events which have such potential impact upon the organism that a reconsideration of strategy is required.

The jurisdiction and scope of comprehensive planning is most firmly established in the military services and in business. From earliest times, planning has been recognized as an integral part of military organizations and operations. And commencing about twenty-five years ago in the United States, corporate planning has become an established managerial function in most large companies and many smaller ones. Successful completion of larger, technically complex projects by the military services, business, and government has always required comprehensive project planning or its equivalent under another name.

Many civil governmental departments and agencies plan their own activities comprehensively. But at the topmost level of federal, state, and local governments, legislatures and chief executives have yet to recognize and establish comprehensive planning as a distinctive and desirable managerial activity integrating and projecting the many constituent activities for which they are responsible. Neither the U.S. Bureau of Management and Budget nor the Congressional Budget Office are designed and organizationally located to fulfill this need at the federal level. Some of the reasons for this governmental reluctance to acknowledge the value of comprehensive planning are noted in the next section.

With rare exceptions, comprehensive planning cannot be conducted successfully by outside consultants. It must function continuously (Principle 9), with the analytical representation of the entirety close at hand and up-to-date (Principle 8). It involves the most critical facts and analysis concerning the organism as a whole, the most sensitive considerations and concerns of top management. Some of this information is restricted to the few top executives, government officials, or military commanders who are the chief decision-makers. Some of it may be company confidential, privileged information, or military classified. None of these operational characteristics fit the indirect, removed, and non-continuous nature of outside consultation.

Attempting to delegate comprehensive planning analysis outside the organism also represents abrogation of basic managerial responsibility. Besides the intrinsic ineffectiveness or impossibility of conducting comprehensive analysis away from the center of information and continuous decision-making, relying on outside consultants signifies that the executive competence and commitment necessary for successful comprehensive planning do not exist within the organism.

Paraphrasing Georges Clemenceau's often-quoted remark concerning military generals and war: comprehensive planning is too important [to the organism] to be left to outside consultants. To succeed, it must be conducted internally within the immediate jurisdiction of the organism, by those directly responsible for final decision-making, with analytical support from planning staffs in organizations large enough to need and provide them. This rule for comprehensive planning does not apply to the occasional or repeated use of outside consultants for technical expertise or particular knowledge that is not available within the organism, or for special studies that cannot be properly conducted internally.

Resistance. . . .
1. Act or an insistence of resisting; opposition, passive or active; also, a method of resisting. . . .
2. Power or capacity to resist. . . .
Resist. . . .
1. To withstand, to be proof against, to be able to repel, ward off, prevent, etc. . . . .
2. To oppose by physical, mental, or moral power, to strive against; to exert oneself to counteract, defeat, or frustrate. . . .
4. To withstand the action of; as a metal *resists* acid. . . .

Reality. . . .
1. State, character, quality, or fact of being real, existent, self-existent, or genuine, or of having real being or existence. . . .
2. Someone real or something real or realized; an actual person, event, situation, or the like; an accomplished fact; also, the substance as opposed to the appearance or form of a thing; as, amid the realities of his life; to make one's dream a reality. . . .
5. *Philos.* **a.** That which actually exists; that which is not imagination, fiction, or pretense; that which has objective existence, and is not merely an idea. . . . **b.** That which is absolute or self-existent, as opposed to what is derivative or dependent; that which is ultimate, as opposed to what is merely apparent or phenomenal. . . .

(*Webster's New International Dictionary of the English Language,* Second Edition (Unabridged), 1960, Vol. II, pp. 2121, 2072)

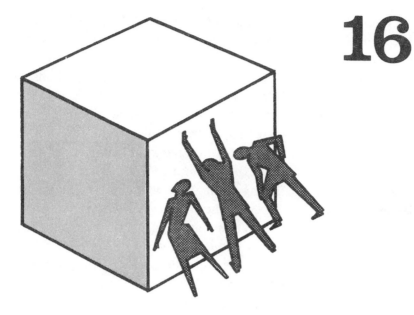

16

RESISTANCE TO PLANNING

Inevitable Reality

PROFESSIONAL PLANNERS ARE KEENLY aware of the frustrations inherent in comprehensive planning. If they are working in a staff capacity, they may wish that they could make the decisions as well as advise those who do. If the planners are government officials, business executives, or commanding officers applying comprehensive planning in their own decision-making—possibly with their own supportive planning staff—they know from experience how slowly desirable improvements can be made.

But at the same time, *planners in general do not realize how basic and inevitable is human resistance to planning and the extent to which it must be taken into account in all such activity,* so much so that it qualifies as a principle of comprehensive planning: "a basic truth, law, or element determining intrinsic nature of characteristic behavior. . . ." Since planning runs counter to several innate characteristics of people, the root of the resistance lies in the nature of humankind and no significant change can therefore be expected in a very long time.

Recognizing and facing reality is fundamental to planning. By definition, it is a process that involves conditions and problems of the real world. But human capacity to face facts and avoid wishful thinking is discouragingly low. People are reluctant to acknowledge unpleasant realities until some circumstance or crisis condition forces recognition. Hope that "springs eternal in the human breast" and illusions are protection against the nagging discomfort of unpleasant truths. Despite the fact that constant awareness of the many pressing problems confronting societies and their implications for the future is more than most people can tolerate, the purpose of comprehensive planning is to identify and evaluate the actual situation however unwanted and unpleasant it may be, to investigate existing problems and formulate recommendations for improvement.

Planning sets aside some of today's resources for use at some future time. This requires people to forego present needs and desires in favor of future benefits which may or may not be attained, and which in any event will be enjoyed by a future generation rather than by those who make the sacrifice today. This renunciation is especially difficult in materialistic societies which lack the motivation for planning provided in the past by some religions which associated abstinences endured on earth with happier life after death. Other religions discourage or restrict planning because of their belief in total predestination which precludes planning since the future is already predetermined by God's will.

> One third of the U.S. population between the ages of 25 and 49 years, are an increasingly gloomy bunch—fretting about their economic status, less willing to make sacrifices for their families and country and more interested in enjoying the present than worrying about the future. (Abrams)

As an aspect of self-preservation—the most fundamental instinct—self-interest is the primary motivation of humankind. Even public-minded individuals active in civic affairs consider their personal interests first and foremost when they believe a proposal admittedly in the general welfare adversely affects their livelihood, family, or some firmly held preference or belief. Myriad special interest groups seek to influence legislation and governmental regulations in their own behalf. Self-concern is inherent in the competitive environment of private enterprise and bureaucratic organization in general. As noted previously (p. 111): "Interservice rivalries long have hindered the making of an integrated military strategy." In general, competitive and conflictive self-interests make comprehensive planning more difficult, unless it is presumed that they combine automatically to produce an overall result that represents the best interest of the organism as a whole.

People prefer certainties to uncertainties: a bird in the hand to several in a plan. In general, they resist change unrelieved by intervals of relative stability, and consider frequent change a sign of poor or at least questionable decision-making. The status quo is the most familiar and comfortable situation. The average individual prefers to plan as little as possible rather than as much as recommended by planners, or even as much as is clearly desirable. For the most part, people's energies are directed to their own personal problems and self-interests. For many the days are consumed with meeting the demands of everyday living which becomes more complicated and time-consuming. Normally, people are concerned with comprehensive planning only when some related development impinges directly on their lives.

Except in dire emergencies, the integration of elements essential in planning does not come easily. Psychologically, people tend to be "lonely islands"; biological and social bases for cooperation develop slowly and often painfully. Coordination implies less selfishness, less egocentrism, willingness to work with others: attributes which it has been amply demonstrated are neither widespread nor readily acquired. Not only coordination but close synthesis are required in comprehensive planning.

Planning presupposes and requires that rationality triumph over irrationality, order over disorder, constructive hope over discouragement and fatalism, action over inaction. It requires extra energy; it is much easier to continue in the existing condition and change only when necessary than to struggle to achieve improvement. Large organizations in particular establish fixed procedures over the years and develop comfortable customs and built-in attitudes which resist inquiry much less change. In addition, planning is analytically exacting requiring the full range of human knowledge; and procedurally difficult to implement because of individual and organizational reluctance to change and undertake steady advance. Like all human activity, planning always operates to someone's disadvantage; there are no plans that benefit everyone equally. Each of these characteristics of the comprehensive planning process makes it harder to establish and perpetuate.

Politics is not only the most important single element of comprehensive governmental planning, but also the chief obstacle to its attainment in the United States. Political decision-makers are more concerned with election to higher office than they are in devoting the time and attention necessary to perform properly in the office they hold. They are reluctant to support comprehensive planning for the organism as a whole when it does not conform to the precise concerns and expressed wishes of their electoral district. They resist the commitments necessary in longer-range planning because they fear that voter attitudes in the future on the issues involved may haunt them at re-election time. As a consequence, comprehensive planning does not yet exist as an effective governmental force in the United States. Those elements of the process that are considered and acted upon legislatively and administratively are uncoordinated and often function at cross purposes.

There are organizational resistances to comprehensive planning as well as those typical of most people as individuals. Political policy and governmental actions in democratic societies are determined by the separate and often differing attitudes and positions of a multitude of organizations, each representing some group of people or institutions. Which of these organizations will combine to initiate or approve a proposed course of action varies with almost every issue, including those related directly and indirectly to comprehensive planning. The groups composing particular coalitions vary over time.

Organizational resistance is more than an accumulation of the reactions of individual people. Its distinctive characteristic is a collective self-interest that is recognized and structured to take political action. The existence of groups of organizations opposing comprehensive planning in whole or in part is inherent in society.

The resistances explained above with reference to civil governmental planning also apply to corporate business and military planning: some to a lesser degree or in another way because of differences between the organisms. The tighter administrative organization of businesses—together with economic, financial, operational, and competitive realities they cannot ignore—reduce wishful thinking and irrational reaction and favor constructive coordination. Obstructive resistances are probably least in military planning because such reactions are severely limited in military organizations. The chain of command constitutes a clear sequence of successive responsibilities for making and carrying out plans, with much less opportunity for individual deviation than in civil governmental and business planning. On the other hand, it is possible that idiosyncratic resistances by individual commanding officers could severely impair military planning and the operational effectiveness of the military organism. Certainly politics exist in one form or another in all human activities. In business and military planning, it is the politics of individual advancement through personal connections that affect comprehensive planning, more than the public politics of elected and appointed government officials.

The difficulties described briefly in this final section do not imply that comprehensive planning is an almost impossible achievement. They do indicate that however great the need it is unrealistic to expect continuous comprehensive planning to be welcomed without question even by those responsible for carrying it out. Resistances to the concept and the process must be anticipated and taken into account when initiating and conducting comprehensive planning. A carefully formulated strategy and deliberate tactics are required.

> Progressive involvement is the key tactic in getting [comprehensive] planning accepted. . . . Item by item, information and analysis are made useful to decision-makers and . . . the powers that be. Their self-interests are deliberately served, with the further purpose of eventually associating these [decision-makers] with the continuous [comprehensive] planning process and staff. First, the information and analysis provided off and on by the planning staff are found reliable and useful by influential individuals. Next, formal procedures are established or

informal ways are found for continuing this staff support. It becomes increasingly difficult for decision-makers to abandon what has become a familiar source of information and analysis. From a small beginning assisting [decision-makers] in connection with their own expressed interests [comprehensive planning] develops gradually until it becomes ingrained as a permanent part of the [organism]. Something of the sort must have occurred in the past preceding the adoption of the budget: at first undoubtedly resisted as an intrusion, now a managerial-administrative fixture that cannot be ignored —although unfortunately it is occasionally manipulated to the point of misrepresentation.   (Branch, 1981)

The realization of comprehensive planning is so difficult—as well as so necessary to institutional success and societal survival —precisely because as one of the highest human achievements it requires extraordinary effort.

References

Abrams, Bill, " 'Middle Generation' Growing More Concerned With Selves," *The Wall Street Journal,* Vol. CXCIX, No. 14, 21 January 1982, p. 25.

Barnard, Chester I. (President, New Jersey Bell Telephone Company), *Methods and Limitations of Foresight in Modern Affairs,* An Address delivered at the Thirtieth Annual Convention of the Association of Life Insurance Presidents, New York, 4 December 1936, pp. 6–7, 2, 4.

Bishop, Jerry E., "U.S. Satellite Data on Soviet Wheat Crop Proved Unusually Accurate, Report Says," *The Wall Street Journal,* Vol. CXCV, No. 95, 14 May 1980, p. 38.

Branch, Melville C., *Continuous City Planning, Integrating Municipal Management and City Planning,* New York (John Wiley & Sons), 1981, pp 60–64; "City Planning Center," pp. 141–159; "Means of Evaluation," pp. 171–173; p. 167.

_____, "The Corporate Representation," in *The Corporate Planning Process,* New York (American Management Association), 1962, pp. 160–167.

Business Week, No. 1955, 12 March 1955, pp. 48, 44.

Churchill, Winston, S., *The Second World War, Their Finest Hour,* Boston (Houghton Mifflin), 1949, p. 402.

Freund, William C., "The Looming Impact of Population Changes," *The Wall Street Journal,* Vol. CVI, No. 66, 6 April 1982, p. 26.

Halloran, Richard, "A Five-Foot Shelf of Iran 'Contingencies,'" *The New York Times,* 18 November 1979, p. 4E; 13 June 1982, P.14Y.

Handler, Philip (President, National Academy of Sciences), in: Large, Arlen J., "The Risk-Benefit Debate," *The Wall Street Journal,* Vol. CXCV, no. 114, 11 June 1980, p. 22.

Haverman, Ernest, "Toughest Cop in the Western World," *Life,* Vol. 36, No. 24, 14 June 1954, p. 133.

Hayes, Thomas C., "Managers Adopting Long-Term Outlook," *The New York Times,* 11 January 1981, XII, p. 40.

Karachi Development Authority, with the assistance of the United Nations, *The Karachi Development Plan 1974–1985,* Final Report, Pilot Project 3, Karachi, Pakistan (Master Plan Department), August 1974, p. vii.

Kester, John G., "Revamp the Joint Chiefs of Staff," *The Wall Street Journal,* Vol. CVI, No. 87, 5 May 1982, p. 26.

Krick, Irving (Consultant, Weather Forecasting; Chief, Weather Information Center, Supreme Headquarters Allied Expeditionary Force), personal communication, 22 May 1982.

Okrent, David, "Comment on Societal Risk," *Science,* Vol. 208, 25 April 1980, p. 372.

Pallot, Judith and Shaw, J. B., *Planning in the Soviet Union,* Athens, Georgia (University of Georgia Press), 1981, p. 256.

Saltzman, Cynthia, "Popes as Patrons: Vatican Art," *The Wall Street Journal,* Vol. CVII, No. 46, 3 September 1982, p. 17.

Smith, Nigel, J. H., "Colonization Lessons from a Tropical Forest," *Science,* Vol. 214, 13 November 1981, pp. 755–761.

Smith, R. Jeoffrey, "An Upheaval in U.S. Strategic Thought," *Science,* Vol. 216, No. 4541, 2 April 1982, p. 34.

Starr, Chauncey, "Social Benefit versus Technological Risk," *Science,* Vol. 165, 19 September 1969, pp. 1232–1238.

The Wall Street Journal, Vol. CVI, No. 33, 18 February 1982, p. 1; No. 64, 2 April 1982, p. 10.

Woolridge, Dean E., "Introduction," in: Branch, Melville C., *The Corporate Planning Process,* New York (American Management Association), 1962, pp. 14, 15.

Zarnowitz, Victor, "Econometric Models Are Shapely, But Rather Dense," *The New York Times,* Sunday, 26 October 1980, Section 4, p. 20E.

INDEX

Abrams, Bill, 193, 197
Ambiguity, 157–158. *See also* Uncertainty

Barnard, Chester I., 31, 32, 82, 197
Branch, Melville C., 74, 128, 197, 198
Business planning. *See* Corporate/Business planning
Business Week, 62, 198

Change, 55–70
 human, 63–66: desires, 65–66; limitations, 63, 64; priorities, 63–65
 natural, 55–62: applicability, 58; environmental effects and planning, 61–62; examples, 56; induced, 58; institutional, 60–61; limitations, 56–57; rate, 59–60, scope, 57
 purposive, 66–70: limitations, 67–68; nature of, 66–67; optimization, 68–70
Churchill, Winston S., 31, 32, 172, 198
Civil governmental plannning, 155–156, 157, *See also* relevant primary headings
Comprehensive planning. *See* Process, plans: comprehensive
Context, open-end, 115–118: analytical completeness, 117–118;

interconnections, 116–118; pitfalls, 116–118
Corporate/Business planning, 12, 25–26, 117, 139, 186. *See also* Process

Definitions. *See* Terms, planning

Elements, primary, 81–97: correlation, 88–89; determination, 83–84, 85–87; integration: evaluation 83, judgmental 93–96; interrelationships, 89–91; selection, 82–83; significance, relative, 92–98; statement, numerical, 96

Feedback, 143–148: comprehensive planning 145; immediate and continuous, 146–147; periodic, 145; real-time, 144
Finer, Herman, 15, 32
Flexibility, 162–165; definition/illustration, 162–164; forms, 164; variation, 164–165

Halloran, Richard, 38, 126, 198
Hayek, Frederick A., 15, 32
Hayes, Thomas C., 25,32

Information, use, 35–43: analysis, limitations, 43; comparability, 41; examples, 36: form, 36–37; graphical, 43; long-range, 38; meaningfulness, 41;